# VOICE OF A PROPHET

# A.W. TOZER

Compiled and Edited by James L. Snyder

# VOICE
## OF A
# PROPHET

## WHO SPEAKS FOR GOD?

BETHANYHOUSE
a division of Baker Publishing Group
Minneapolis, Minnesota

© 2014 by James L. Snyder

Published by Bethany House Publishers
11400 Hampshire Avenue South
Bloomington, Minnesota 55438
www.bethanyhouse.com

Bethany House Publishers is a division of
Baker Publishing Group, Grand Rapids, Michigan

Bethany House edition published 2014
ISBN 978-0-7642-1626-8

Previously published by Regal Books

Printed in the United States of America

The Library of Congress has cataloged the original edition as follows:
Tozer, A. W. (Aiden Wilson), 1897-1963.
    Voice of a prophet / A.W. Tozer.
      pages cm
    ISBN 978-0-8307-7026-7 (trade paper)
      1. Prophecy—Christianity. 2. Prophets—Calling of. 3. Church. I. Title.
BR115.P8T69 2014
231.7'45—dc23                                        2013051228

Scripture quotations are from the King James Version of the Bible.

15   16   17   18   19   20   21        8   7   6   5   4   3   2

# CONTENTS

# THE PRAYER OF A
# MINOR PROPHET

When A. W. Tozer was just beginning his preaching ministry, he was interviewed for ordination by a group of elders and ministers. Up to this point, he had been preaching on street corners, under gospel tents and now in a little storefront church in the hills of West Virginia. After interviewing him, the group of elders met together and all came to one conclusion: This man was not ready to be ordained; he had never finished high school; he had never attended a Bible college or seminary; he had no training whatsoever in ministry.

The men had almost come to the point of refusing to ordain Tozer when one man spoke out and said, "This man has a real passion for ministry; and even though he has no college education or ministry training, I think we ought to give him a try."

Reluctantly, they agreed to the ordination.

Granted, Tozer did not fit the ministry template of his day. I am sure he would not fit today's template, either.

The prophet God uses is uniquely called of God. He never volunteers for the job. He is called. Think of the lives of such biblical prophets as Elijah, Elisha and even John the Baptist. Think of David. Nobody thought David the shepherd could be king, but he turned out to be the greatest king Israel ever had.

A. W. Tozer was sort of like David. Few people thought he would ever amount to anything in the ministry, and yet he became one of the leading voices of his generation, with a message that continues even to this day to those who have ears to hear.

It was not man's approval that made Dr. Tozer the prophet of his day; it was God's call—His choosing of a man who was willing to be used of God. It is impossible to define that "call." I think Tozer would agree when I say that those who seem right for the job are not the ones God calls. God chooses a man or a woman who is out of sync with his or her generation. God uses a person, not because he or she fits in, but usually because he or she does not fit in.

After the elders and ministers had prayed and laid hands on him, Tozer withdrew to meet his Savior in the secret place and the silence, farther in than his well-meaning brethren could take him. Tozer wrote down the prayer that was his covenant with God. Thirty years later, he published it in the magazine he edited, *The Alliance Witness,* and called it "The Prayer of a Minor Prophet." This prayer has been published many times. Its words reveal the heartbeat of a man God can use.

O Lord, I have heard Thy voice and was afraid. Thou hast called me to an awesome task in a grave and perilous hour. Thou art about to shake all nations and the earth and also heaven that the things that cannot be shaken may remain. O Lord, my Lord, Thou hast stooped to honor me to be Thy servant. No man taketh this honor upon himself save he that is called of God as was Aaron. Thou hast ordained me, Thy messenger to them that are stubborn of heart and hard of hearing. They have rejected Thee, the Master, and it is not to be expected that they will receive me, the servant.

My God, I shall not waste time deploring my weakness nor my unfittedness for the work. The responsibility is not mine, but Thine. Thou hast said, "I knew thee—I ordained thee—I sanctified thee," and Thou hast also said, "Thou shalt go to all that I shall send thee, and whatsoever I command thee thou shalt speak." Who am I to argue with Thee or to call into question Thy sovereign choice? The decision is not mine, but Thine. So be it, Lord. Thy will, not mine, be done.

Well do I know, Thou God of the prophets and the apostles, that as long as I honor Thee, Thou wilt honor me. Help me, therefore, to take this solemn vow to honor Thee in all my future life and labors— whether by gain or by loss, by life or by death—and then to keep that vow unbroken while I live.

It is time, O God, for Thee to work, for the enemy has entered into Thy pastures, and the sheep are torn and scattered. False shepherds abound who deny the danger and laugh at the perils which surround Thy flock. The sheep are deceived by these hirelings and follow them with touching loyalty while the wolf closes in to kill and destroy. I beseech Thee, give me sharp eyes to detect the presence of the enemy; give me understanding to see, and courage to faithfully report what I see. Make my voice so like Thine own that even the sick sheep will recognize it and follow Thee.

Lord Jesus, I come to Thee for spiritual preparation. Lay Thy hand upon me. Anoint me with the oil of the New Testament prophet. Forbid that I should become a religious scribe and thus lose my prophetic calling. Save me from the curse that lies dark across the modern clergy: the curse of compromise, of imitation, of professionalism. Save me from the error of judging a church by its size, its popularity or the amount of its yearly offering. Help me to remember that I am a prophet—not a promoter, not a religious manager, but a prophet. Let me never become a slave to crowds. Heal my soul of carnal ambitions and deliver me from the itch for publicity.

Save me from bondage to things. Let me not waste my days puttering around the house. Lay Thy terror upon me, O God, and drive me to the place of prayer where I may wrestle with principalities and powers and the rulers of the darkness of this world. Deliver me from overeating and late sleeping. Teach me self-discipline that I may be a good soldier of Jesus Christ.

I accept hard work and small rewards in this life. I ask for no easy place. I shall try to be blind to the little ways that could make life easier. If others seek the smoother path, I shall try to take the hard way without judging them too harshly. I shall expect opposition and try to take it quietly when it comes. Or if, as sometimes falleth out to Thy servants, I should have grateful gifts pressed upon me by Thy kindly people, stand by me then and save me from the blight that often follows. Teach me to use whatever I receive in such manner that will not injure my soul nor diminish my spiritual power. And if, in Thy permissive providence, honor should come to me from Thy church, let me not forget in that hour that I am unworthy of the least of Thy mercies, and that if men knew me as intimately as I know myself, they would withhold their honors or bestow them upon others more worthy to receive them.

And now, O Lord of heaven and earth, I consecrate my remaining days to Thee; let them be many or few, as Thou wilt. Let me stand before the great, or minister to the poor and lowly; that choice is not mine, and I would not influence it if I could. I am Thy servant to do Thy will, and that will is sweeter to me than position or riches or fame; and I choose it above all things on earth or in heaven.

Though I am chosen of Thee and honored by a high and holy calling, let me never forget that I am but a man of dust and ashes, a man with all the natural faults and passions that plague the race of men. I pray Thee, therefore, my Lord and Redeemer, save me from myself and from all the injuries I may do myself while trying to be a blessing to others. Fill me with Thy power by the Holy Spirit, and I will go in Thy strength and tell of Thy righteousness, even Thine only. I will spread abroad the message of redeeming love while my normal powers endure.

Then, dear Lord, when I am old and weary and too tired to go on, have a place ready for me above, and make me to be numbered with Thy saints in glory everlasting. Amen. AMEN.

Throughout the years, Dr. Tozer renewed this covenant with God. It is the one document he carried with him always.

This book is based upon a variety of sermons Dr. Tozer preached on the subject of a prophet and his work. The church today is in desperate need of the kind of prophet Dr. Tozer describes. Using the lives of such biblical prophets as Elijah, Elisha and even John the Baptist, this book underscores the utter importance of the ministry of the prophet in today's church.

The ministry of a prophet far exceeds his generation. The validity of a prophet is seen in his message, which transcends generations; although the messenger is physically gone, the message remains vital. May God raise up more prophets to speak the message in our generation and beyond.

James L. Snyder

# VOICE

OF A

# PROPHET

# 1

# WHOSE CHURCH IS IT, REALLY?

*And the sons of the prophets that were at Bethel came forth*
*to Elisha, and said unto him, Knowest thou that the LORD*
*will take away thy master from thy head to day? And he said,*
*Yea, I know it; hold ye your peace.*

2 KINGS 2:3

Anyone who is familiar with my sermons, my books or editorials will attest to the fact that the great passion of my life is God. I make no bones about it; I am absolutely devoted to pursuing God each day of my life—to make God the focus of everything I do.

This has cost me down through the years. Many members of my family and my friends have misunderstood me, and I have had to choose between God and family and friends. I think I can safely say that my one passion is pursuing God.

Years ago, I was having lunch with Dr. H. M. Shuman, then president of the Christian and Missionary Alliance. I was a young pastor at the beginning stage of my ministry. We talked about a few things, and then, at an appropriate pause in the conversation, I told Dr. Shuman that I wanted to love God more than anyone loved God of my generation.

I meant every word of it. Of course, at the time, I genuinely did not know what it all meant.

Dr. Shuman just stared at me for a few moments and then very carefully said, "Brother Tozer, if that is the true desire of your heart, I have one word of caution: Prepare yourself to suffer greatly."

I took to heart what he said, and down through the years, the truth of that warning has unfolded itself in many ways. Indeed, it has cost greatly for me to put God first in my life; but I must say, at this point of my life, it certainly has been well worth it.

I have made many stumbles and bumbles, but I have tried to the best of my ability to keep God as the very focus of my life.

The second great passion of my heart is the church of Jesus Christ, particularly the evangelical/fundamentalist church. I have done a great deal of ministry among this Body of Christ. I think I can honestly say that I love them with a godly love.

Because I love them with a godly love, I need to address certain problems that have been developing for several generations. I saw one church advertise that they were "Not your father's church." They promoted it as though they were proud of that expression. What I want to know is, if they are "Not your father's church," whose church are they?

## The Church Incognito

It is my humble opinion that when a person loses sight of the origins of the Church, it no longer is the Church. Therefore, the question is, what is it?

Have we come to a stage in this generation that the so-called church is promoting everything and anything that will add to its numbers? The bottom line, as they say, is success; and success has everything to do with numbers. Whatever brings the numbers in must be all right.

This is far from the church fathers who gave their lives to establish the church of Jesus Christ.

The problem, as I see it, is that we have lost the vision the fathers had of what we refer to as the New Testament church.

One of the main factors of the New Testament church is the prophets. They were used of God to lead the church through tumultuous times and prevent her from falling into heresies. Heresies began almost the day the church was born.

When you read through the New Testament and follow up with the early history of the church, you can see that the church was successful as they listened to the voice of the prophets. When they turned a deaf ear to that voice, the church quickly sank into heresies. Some of those heresies linger on to this day.

My great passion and love for the church leads me to cry out in desperation that what we need today are prophets. Where are the prophets to guide today's church through the quagmire of heresies around us?

Those early church prophets were successful to the degree that the church listened to them.

The voice of the prophet today is seldom heard, not because there are no prophets speaking for God, but because the noise and clatter of our culture have so invaded the church that they have drowned out that voice. Because the voice is not being heard, the church is in danger of falling into the quagmire of heresy.

What has brought the church to this point?

## Like Father, Unlike Son

I believe one dangerous factor today is the sons of the prophets. This seems to be where our generation has come. The prophets are in the background, but the sons are in the forefront. Even though these sons have a connection with the fathers, they do not seem to be like their fathers.

Every generation seems to drift a little further away from the vision of what God has for the church.

These sons of the prophets, who have a vague, if any, connection with the past, are now running the church. Today it is quite popular to distance yourself from the past. If someone sees in you some connection to the past, you are ridiculed to the point of turning your back on the past.

When the church turns her back on the past, she has no sense of her future. She is like a ship without a rudder, floundering in a vast sea of uncertainty.

Several characteristics about these sons of the prophets concern me, and because of my great love for the church, I need to speak out.

### Promote Marketing over Message

Perhaps at the top of the list would be the awful truth that they are not message oriented. The message is not really that important. What is being touted today to run the church is marketing, presentation of the message, and performance. These three things have overshadowed the message.

When the prophets were running things, it was the message that really mattered. If you look at the prophets, as we shall in this book, you can see they were all different. There is no prototype. There are no cookie-cutter prophets. The only thing that was important about them was the message they brought, and that message had better be of God.

The warning in the Old Testament concerning false prophets should be alarming to us. If the prophet's message did not come to pass, that was a sign of a false prophet. The whole thing had to do with the message: "When a prophet speaketh in the name of the LORD, if the thing follow not, nor come to pass, that *is* the thing which the LORD hath not spoken, *but* the prophet hath spoken it presumptuously: thou shalt not be afraid of him" (Deut. 18:22).

Today, it is hard to see what the message is because of all of the accoutrements around the message. It has come to the point of not being recognized from a biblical standpoint.

In some places, the church is being marketed as though it were a business. Christianity is not a commercial commodity or product. I do not see that in the New Testament.

What bothers me is the fact that the message gives way and takes second place to the presentation of the message. If the message is presented in a certain way, it is okay regardless if some point is missing. That is my definition of heresy. Heresy is presenting truth but conveniently leaving out some of the truth. This is happening today through the presentation process we have today.

Today many people are taking the message for granted. The message has lost its meaning over time. With these sons of the prophets, the message has not cost them anything, and for many they have become bored with the message and are trying to jazz it up somehow.

To become bored with the message is the tragedy the church is facing today.

### Give Cultural Relevancy First Priority

There is a passion today to be relevant. This, I believe, is one of the gods of the modern church. We will go to great lengths to prove that the message fits in nicely with the culture around us.

The sons of the prophets assume that their interpretation or presentation of the message is the only correct one. To them it is important to interpret the message in such a way as to fit present circumstances and culture. They do not want to do anything that would cause any harm or embarrassment to the culture around them. I think G. K. Chesterton was right when he said, "Therefore it is the paradox of history that each generation is converted by the saint who contradicts it most." And yet, to understand the message is to understand how devastating the message is on the culture of any generation, whether it be the New Testament church age or our age today. The message contradicts our culture in every aspect.

Some of this has come by way of modern Bible translations. In my study, I have every Bible translation ever published. Care must be taken that the translation does not adversely affect the message. After all, the message is the thing that is really important. Have we come to the point in the church where the most important thing is the messenger and not the message? We will accept the message in any form as long as we approve of the messenger. The spotlight is now on the messenger, and at best the message has taken second place.

In all of this, the emphasis is on the peripheral elements or aspects of the message. These sons of the prophets rarely get to the heart of the gospel message. Happy are they to present aspects of the message that can be endorsed by anybody and everybody.

## How to Disguise the Full Message

Three elements are present here: sensationalism, emotionalism and entertainment. I must point out that all these are contrary to wholesome spiritual development.

### Make It Sensational

Sensationalism can capture the headlines, so to speak. That is just a temporary thing. When we sensationalize the gospel message, we out of necessity must take it out of context. There was nothing sensational about dying on the cross. To try to sensationalize this is to miss the whole focus of the crucifixion. To turn the crucifixion into entertainment is about as blasphemous as you can get.

### Make It Emotional

I have seen some of these sons of the prophets stir up an audience emotionally. By playing on their emotions, they can control the audience and bring that audience to any point they want to. We used to see this in the circus; now we are seeing it in the pulpit. Can anything be more blasphemous than that?

What most people do under an emotional high will never translate into daily disciplined living for God.

### Make It Entertaining

The thing I cannot understand or accept is the entertainment aspect of today's sons of the prophets. For some reason, they go to Hollywood to get their authority these days. If they can only package the message in an acceptable manner that will entertain the most numbers of people, they count that to be successful. Even so, I wonder how entertaining it was for Jesus to die on the cross?

How entertaining was it for Stephen, the first martyr, to die in the presence of his enemies? How entertaining was it for the martyrs of the church to march into their martyrdom? Who was applauding all of this? Who was being entertained by the sufferings and sacrifices of the saints of the church?

All of this is contrary to wholesome spiritual development. The sons of the prophets have created a generation of pseudo-Christians that bear little or no resemblance to those early Christians who died for their faith.

In all of this, the sons of the prophets are careful to leave out any offensive parts. They are very selective about the truth they present. What they present is true, but what they leave out is devastating.

It seems that every denomination has cherry-picked the truth of the message they will focus on. To cherry-pick means that some truth is unaccounted for, which means the message is incomplete.

Under the sons of the prophets, I think the message has lost its sharpness. There seems to be no condemnation element in the church anymore. Conviction has lost its place, and nobody is calling the church to repentance. There is nothing to repent for anymore. We are God's happy, happy little children, dancing our way into heaven. What a pathetic description.

Nowadays, the messenger is more important than the message. The message depends upon celebrities to carry it into the culture. No other generation needed celebrities. Could it be that the Holy Spirit is not as necessary today? Could it be that we need help from celebrities, especially those who have never experienced a life-changing relationship with Jesus Christ and have a lifestyle completely contrary to biblical standards?

In order to enlist the celebrities, the message needs to be watered down and modified so that it is not quite as sharp and the celebrity is the focal point of the message.

Under the leadership of the sons of the prophets, I have noticed that hands have become soft while hearts have become hard.

Everybody will admit to making some "mistake." After all, nobody's perfect, right? But where is that Christian who will stand up as the tax collector of old and beat his breast and say, "God be merciful unto me a sinner"?

Today we say we have "missed the mark," "not been up to our potential," "tried to make it the best we can." I have heard all of these psychological excuses, and they are coming from our sons of the prophets.

## Back to the Whole Message

When will we come to the point of repentance, throw all the excuses out the window and fall on our faces before God and an open Bible? When will we repent of our sin and allow the Holy Spirit to do whatever the Holy Spirit wants to do?

We have bred a generation that is far removed from the forefathers and is almost indistinguishable as being related to them. We have a generation of sons of the prophets that is more interested in the accoutrements of the message than in the inner reality of the message.

This generation has forgotten that the message does not clean up and shine the outside of a person; rather, it bores into the very heart and core of a person and radically changes that person from the inside.

The time has come to hear once again the voice of God through His prophets. A prophet is not cultivated; a prophet is called and sent by God. One of my passions is to see God once again in the center of His church—to see Him honored and glorified in such a manner that it will push out all the things that are contrary to the holiness of God.

*O, God, God of the prophets of old, fall upon us in our utter weakness and radically transform Your Church today. In Jesus' name. Amen.*

# 2

# THE BLIGHT OF
# TODAY'S CHURCH

*Beloved, believe not every spirit, but try the spirits whether they are
of God: because many false prophets are gone out into the world.*

1 JOHN 4:1

The warning against false prophets started back in
the days of the New Testament church. All of the
apostles warned the church concerning these coming false prophets that would prey upon the church, especially upon new Christians.

What makes the New Testament so relevant today is
that the church today is facing the same problems the early
church faced in the days of its infancy. I can think of no
problem we face but what was addressed by one of the New
Testament apostles.

This present generation, however, believes that they have
new problems. My contention, however, is simply that every
problem has a spiritual origin and can be traced back to the
New Testament warnings.

Granted, there never has been a climate more hospitable to the uprising of the false prophets. And with the increase of media outlets like those we have today, these problems are brought into the home.

Along these lines, my concern is that the proliferation of false prophets has compromised the true meaning of God to our generation. We are allowing preachers to preach without any accountability whatsoever. Even when a preacher is proven to be a scoundrel, he continues to influence without any kind of hindrance whatsoever. The ones who are affected by these false prophets are those who are not rooted and grounded in scriptural teaching.

As the apostle John warned, "Believe not every spirit" (1 John 4:1). Has there ever been a generation as gullible as those today who will believe anything they read or hear in the newspaper, radio or television?

The church used to deal with these false prophets by a mighty move of God, which some refer to as revival. What we desperately need today is another revival, but I do not see one on the horizon. I pray for it constantly. I hope for it now more than ever. And God knows, we desperately need it today.

In reading the history of revivals, it seems to me that the present generation is primed for a revival. I think that would clear the deck for the next generation.

## Signs of a False Prophet

False prophets, since the days of the early church, have made insidious inroads into the church. By the time a false prophet is recognized as a false prophet, he or she has caused considerable harm to the church. I need not outline that sort of thing from church history; every cult in the world today began with a false prophet in the church.

Several things about a false prophet need to be understood and watched for in the church today.

### Promotes Self

Perhaps the worst thing that I could say about these false prophets is that they malign God's character in order to promote themselves. This is the first warning we need to take care of.

When God's character is at stake, we need to be very careful. Our God is a holy God and will not stand for His character to be maligned by malicious false prophets trying to gain a personal advantage.

An old preacher once said that if you want to become famous and rich, get into the church. Of course, he was referring to false prophets who have gorged themselves with the tithes and offerings of God's weak sheep.

Many a preacher has gone into the ministry and sacrificed everything for the work of God. These servants need to be honored and revered throughout their lifetime. But many who enter into the ministry do it for gain. They have a personal agenda they want to pursue, and they find that the best way to do that is through some religious content.

To malign God's character begins with not really understanding the God of the Bible. Everybody is religious and everybody has a religious opinion about everything in the Bible. Everybody thinks they know who God is, and some have referred to Him as the "One up there that likes me."

I hate that phrase because it has nothing to do with the God of the Bible.

To take the character of God and twist it in such a way as to make God out to be someone He is not must be condemned for what it is. To redefine God in terms that help someone's personal agenda can only be called blasphemous.

The fact that God allows this has always been a mystery to me and has been an incentive to focus on who is the God of the Bible. I have a passion to know God; and when someone makes a caricature out of God, it drives me to my knees. I often pray, "I cannot answer that man, but I know Thee."

I want to know God, and I want to know God in such a way that I can introduce Him to those who also long to know God. I do not want anybody messing with the biblical description of God. I do not want anybody twisting the character of God into a caricature.

Self-promotion should be reprimanded by all concerned. Unfortunately, most of these false prophets are not accountable to anybody who is able to curtail their activities. Hence, we have an ongoing flow of thoughts and ideas about God that is at complete odds with the biblical description of God. The sons of the prophets are enabling these false prophets.

### Cherry-picks and Distorts the Message

We also find that these false prophets pick and choose what they want to believe about God. They want to believe in the love of God, but they do not want to believe in the wrath of God. They pick out all of the biblical descriptions about the love of God, and create an untrue picture of God, because you cannot have a picture of God that is incomplete. Their ideas of God are so far out of balance that they lead people away from the true God.

Based upon that, the next level of a false prophet is that he distorts God's message. This is a critical issue. I want to know what God is saying, and I want to have it deeply rooted in biblical evidence. I do not want somebody's commentary on what the Bible says. I want to know what the Bible says "other than by hearsay," as Thomas Carlyle stated it.

If you get two people to describe a picture, they will come up with two different descriptions. One may leave one detail out and the other will leave out something else. To really understand that picture, you have to see the picture yourself. I think that when we come to the Word of God, we need to know what the Word of God says.

We need to be more like the Berean Christians, as Paul put it: "These were more noble than those in Thessalonica, in that they received the word with all readiness of mind, and searched the scriptures daily, whether those things were so" (Acts 17:11). Paul warned the Christians not to take even his word, but to search the Scriptures to make sure that what he was saying was true. We need more of this today.

These false prophets distort God's message by making the messenger more important than the message. Here again, we are turning the messenger into a celebrity.

It's common to say, "Let us go hear so-and-so," as though that preacher is better than any other preacher around. It is not the messenger; it is the message that needs to be proclaimed.

If you study the Old and New Testaments, you will soon discover that no prophet can ever become a celebrity.

The most significant thing about the prophet is the message he conveys, and that message had better be rooted in the heart of God.

I love what Charles H. Spurgeon's grandfather, who was also a preacher, said of his grandson: "Charles can preach the gospel better than me, but he cannot preach a better gospel." We are called to preach the gospel. The vehicle that brings the gospel is only a vehicle and must be worthy of the gospel he is bringing.

False prophets have a way of twisting the message just enough to fool the shallow Christian. If 99 percent of what a false prophet says is true, it is a given that he is a true prophet. However, the 1 percent disqualifies that man from being a true prophet of God. Either it is all the way or it is no way.

It is amazing to me how clever false prophets are in twisting the message in such a way as to fool the majority of Christians. Just enough twist to make it sound right. If a person is a Bible student and follower of the Lord Jesus Christ, and open to the work of the Holy Spirit, these false prophets will not fool him.

"Try the spirits," said the apostle John, because he knew that there were many false prophets who would hover over the flock of God to take advantage of them and prey upon them in such a manner as to dishonor the glory of God.

The end result of these false prophets is that they confuse God's sheep. This is the burden of my heart, particularly for the new Christian as well as the shallow Christian. I wish that all Christians had a heart for God that would push them beyond the agendas of some of these false prophets and into the very heart of God Himself.

What these false prophets do is rob Christians of God's best. I need to remind God's people that God has our best interests in mind for the longest period of time. God allows certain things to happen in our lives because there is a bigger picture in mind and God is taking us through those experiences.

The false prophet would tell you that if you are a Christian you should not experience any bad times. Everything should go wonderfully for you. You should prosper and be successful in everything you touch your hand to. That sounds fine, but it has no root in the Word of God. What it does do is take the focus off what God has for us.

Robbing God's people of God's best is one of the fundamental problems in this generation. These false prophets are exchanging God's best for what they consider their best. Are we followers of God, or are we following man? False prophets would have us follow them. Always remember that when you follow a man, he will always lead you away from God.

## Leads in the Wrong Direction

This brings me to the point that false prophets lead people the wrong way. Maybe these false prophets have been deceived themselves. Maybe they believe what they are saying. Maybe they are being used by the enemy of man's soul and do not even know it. I do not know if I could tell the difference; all I know is that they are leading people away from God.

It is my passion to lead people *to* God. That is where they belong. That is what they were created for. St. Augustine had it right when he pronounced, "Thou, O God, hast created us for Thyself, and we are restless until we rest in Thee." To do less is to rob people of what God created them for in the very beginning.

In order for these false prophets to keep the people following them, they must feed them with spiritually toxic food. This toxic food is a little bit of psychology, a little bit of inspiration, a dash of theology, a touch of Bible and a whole lot of personality.

Each of these false prophets has his own recipe for this toxic food. I am not sure, but perhaps Solomon had this in mind when he wrote, "And further, by these, my son, be admonished: of making many books there is no end; and much study is a weariness of the flesh" (Eccles. 12:12).

I wonder if Solomon saw the stream of these toxic books flooding this generation. The church is being flooded with books that are adversely affecting a whole generation of Christians.

Every false prophet has a book that rises just a wee bit higher than the Bible, and he is very careful in marketing this book so the average shallow Christian will not notice this.

## Majors in Minors

One other aspect of the false prophet is that he overwhelms God's people with trivia. Never has there been more trivia flowing into the church than today. Much of this trivia is coming from the world and into the church without anyone stopping it anywhere.

I want to know, where are the gatekeepers? Where are the watchmen concerned about what is coming into the church? As watchmen, we have lost ground in this regard.

God warned the Old Testament saints, "So thou, O son of man, I have set thee a watchman unto the house of Israel; therefore thou shalt hear the word in my mouth and warn them from me" (Ezek. 33:7).

Where are these watchmen? Where are these prophets warning God's people of the false prophets invading God's territory?

It has come to the point that if any preacher criticizes any movement, he is quickly ostracized and made fun of. However, it is our responsibility—our job—to point out these false prophets, whether other people listen to us or not.

God's instruction to the prophet was, "Nevertheless, if thou warn the wicked of his way to turn from it; if he do not turn from his way, he shall die in his iniquity; but thou hast delivered thy soul" (Ezek. 33:9).

The responsibility of the prophet is not to come up with his own message but to faithfully deliver the message, the warning that is coming from God. If the people hear and turn from their wicked ways, then God will bless them. If they do not listen, do not turn from their wicked ways, it is not the responsibility of the prophet. He has done his job, and the rest is up to God.

We must give warning concerning the false prophets that are gaining such ground among the people of God. We must warn the people about those who are turning them away from the true God. If they hear us, we can praise God. If they do not hear us, we can mourn for them but know that we have done our job.

*Our heavenly Father, how grateful we are that You have given a message, and then given a voice to that message, to the prophets You have chosen. May those prophets be sent, and may Thy people turn from their wicked ways to serve Thee today. Amen.*

# 3

# God's Message to His Church

*Now go, write it before them in a table, and note it in a book,*
*that it may be for the time to come for ever and ever.*

ISAIAH 30:8

The true prophet is called to be a voice of God to his generation. His mission is to bring God's message to God's people, in such a way that they hear it and obey it. Therefore, he needs to be rooted deeply in the Word of God.

What is the purpose and mission of the Word of God? To find us, to locate us—to identify us and our times—and to reveal truth to us. Its purpose is to show what is wrong with us, but also to show what is right with us.

## God's Message Is Not for Everyone

One thing that is often overlooked is that the prophet has no message to the world. The prophet brings God's Word and message to God's people. God's message through His prophets has always been directed to His people and their overall well-being. This positive aspect of prophecy is often overlooked.

As a result of all the damage false prophets have done and are doing to the church of God, there is a tendency to concentrate on the negative. Surely, we must point out those things that are wrong, and the Word of God is faithful in showing us what is wrong about us. But you cannot have a positive without a negative. Both sides are needed.

I am often accused of being negative, but that does not trouble me in the least. Many try to be 100 percent positive, which is an absolute impossibility.

It does not matter how bad a person is—it does not matter what he has done throughout his life; you can always discover something good about that person. This is true for the other side as well. There is always something negative about the person who believes he is entirely positive.

## What the Message Achieves

Now, the work of the prophet is to convey God's Word to God's people in the proper balance. God never says anything negative to His people but what He also presents the positive side. We are to deal with the negative, but we are to focus on what is right about our walk with God.

It does not matter if things are either negative or positive in the world. Out in the world, people are lost, and until they come to faith in Jesus Christ, God has nothing really to say about them. They are headed for judgment to come.

In the church, it is a different story. Regardless of how badly a person has backslidden, God always has a way to come back prepared for him or her. Nobody has ever done anything that was a surprise to God.

I am sure that it did not shock God when Adam and Eve did what they did in the Garden of Eden. He was not standing in the heavens rubbing His hands together, worrying about what He would do next. God's plan is always built in eternity and cannot be destroyed by time.

The apostle John pointed to this truth in the book of Revelation with these words: "The book of life of the Lamb slain from the foundation of the world" (Rev. 13:8). Before God had even created the heavens and the earth, the Lamb of God had already offered the sacrifice for sins to come.

## What the Message Contains

Part of the message of the prophet is to show God's people what they are doing right and what impact it is having upon the world around them.

We do not often think about the fact that God takes great delight in His people. I believe that God is filled with laughter as He takes delight in His redeemed people. He delights in the ones created in His image who have now been redeemed and brought back to that image and are growing in the grace and knowledge of the Lord Jesus Christ. The heavens are filled with the laughter of God as He delights in His people.

I have come across some Christians who constantly beat themselves over the head about the least little thing. Some of these people are afraid to say anything good about themselves for fear they are violating some aspect of humility, a characteristic they grossly misunderstand. They are the saddest people you would ever want to see. Being around them brings you down several layers of sadness. Why Christians should be sad is beyond me. We should be the most joyful people on God's green earth.

The job of a good medical doctor is not only to find what is wrong with your health but also to encourage you when you are doing okay health-wise. Likewise, the business of the Word of God is to tell you when you are wrong, but also to tell you when you are right, and say, "Well done, go ahead, my child."

There is no virtue in always condemning yourself, because the Word of God shows us what is right in us as well as what is wrong. Now, let me be clear that there is nothing right about a sinner; there is nothing right about a lost man; nothing right about a rebel against God. And I think it is safe to say that there is nothing right about the popular religion as we know it today. All of this is entirely in sync with the prophet's message.

But the prophet is not always bringing bad news; he also brings words of encouragement that keep us in fellowship with God. Sometimes we need encouragement, and God is faithful in bringing encouragement into our lives through the voice of a prophet.

## The Prophet Is Only the Messenger

The will of God is the health of the universe. God is the harmony of heaven. He is the peace of Paradise. The will of God is salvation itself. The will of God is light. The will of God is everything a moral being can want.

Keeping all of that in mind, the prophet's message is not, and cannot be, a personal diatribe. Study the prophets of the Old Testament and you will see that the message did not originate with them. They were not giving a message because they had a little chip on their shoulder and wanted to give God's people a piece of their mind.

The message never originates with the prophet. It is God's job to connect the prophet with the message He wants to impart to His people. It is never left up to the prophet.

Martin Luther set the standard when he declared, "Here I stand; I can do no other. God help me. Amen!" Luther could not and would not change the message, regardless of personal consequences.

The message does not originate with a prophet and, therefore, cannot be modified by the prophet. The prophet's sole responsibility is to deliver God's message just the way God gave it.

To do this, a prophet needs to be uniquely prepared to deliver the message. God does not simply pluck someone out of the back hills without his being uniquely prepared for a unique work. Not just anyone can be God's prophet. (And nobody has ever volunteered to be God's prophet or mouthpiece to a generation.)

This message that God entrusts to His prophet is under strict orders from God, without any deviation. The song of the prophet is, "Thus saith the Lord." Any other song will never do for God's man to be God's voice to his generation.

## God's Message Confronts the Present Situation

One important aspect of the message God gives to the prophet is that it always exploits the condition of God's people. It is not a general message for everybody. Those who have

//

rebelled against God—those who do not own God—receive no message from God except the message of repentance.

God's message through His prophet is always given in the context of the present conditions. It always gives a true picture from God's perspective of the situation. Many times, we can justify certain irregularities and make excuses for it. God's message comes without excuse as a direct word from God about a specific situation.

Keep in mind that the message carries with it God's wisdom and understanding of the present situation. God sees what we cannot see and understands what we will never understand: "For my thoughts are not your thoughts" (Isa. 55:8). God's wisdom is brought to bear upon our situation, and the message given to us through the prophets conveys that wisdom to our situation.

The message God gives always confronts the present condition in order to contradict that situation and move people toward God. God does not condemn just to condemn; He does so in order to turn the situation around and bring the people back to where they need to be—in fellowship with God.

God's message cuts through the smoke and mirrors and brings truth to bear upon that particular situation. God is not just trying to prove that He is right. God has nothing to prove to us. Rather, He draws us back to the position of His divine pleasure. God takes so much delight in us that He will go to any length to bring us back to that delight.

### God's Message Points the Way Back to God

This brings me to the fact that God's message always includes the path back to God. There is only one path back. It is not a variety of choices and options. There is one path back, and God's message always stresses that one way. It is always clearly defined, although it is rarely an easy choice for us.

God's message brings to it an honest evaluation concerning the danger confronting us. God does not have to exaggerate the danger. He never has to underestimate the danger. God always brings to our situation, through the voice of the prophet, an honest evaluation of the situation and how it affects our relationship with God.

### God's Message Costs

The essence of the message of the prophet is truth. Truth is always a double-edged sword. It cuts both ways. There is a cost factor for the prophet to deliver the message, and there is a cost factor for us to receive that message. This emphasizes the extreme importance God puts upon the truth He is trying to bring our way.

When it comes to truth, it must be regarded as not only the will of God but also the heart of God. God is not laying upon us strict disciplines to delight in our suffering. Sometimes we get this idea from people who, for some reason, glorify suffering. I never delight in my suffering. That is why it is called suffering.

God will endure our suffering because he knows the end result will bring us closer to His heart. The way back to God is a difficult one, and not a few stumble along the way. God weeps for those who are stumbling and reaches out through the voice of the prophet to give the guidance necessary for them to get back on their feet again and resume the journey back into the heart of God.

That path back to God's heart is a direct route. God is not taking us through a bunch of side roads just to give us a tour of the scenery. God's path is direct. It starts where we are right now and goes to where He is and where He wants us to be. We are the ones who are responsible for the side trips that have cost us time as well as other things.

I will be the first to admit that the path is always radical. My relationship with Jesus Christ is a radical relationship. It is neither passive nor convenient, but radically focused in the direction of God. Whatever the cost, I gladly bear it and draw nearer to God.

We accept radical behavior in many areas of human endeavor. Why can't we accept radical behavior in a heart that is panting and longing for God? Let us get off the easy train ride, with all of the beautiful scenery, and get back on that radical path that leads directly into the heart of our Father, who art in heaven.

## Requirement: Radical Faith

I also need to point out that this path is nonnegotiable. "And thine ears shall hear a word behind thee, saying, This *is* the way, walk ye in it, when ye turn to the right hand, and when ye turn to the left" (Isa. 30:21). God has established a path, and we either accept that path or we do not end up with God. God is not interested in negotiating in this area. We are a generation of negotiators. We want to give a little here and get a little there, thinking we can bring this method into our relationship with God. God is God, and He allows for no negotiations.

The path back to God is not dependent upon our understanding it. It begins in faith and continues in faith. Often, it is referred to as a walk of faith. In this walk of faith, our focus has to be on God, who is calling us back to Himself. It is the faithful prophet who points us to the way, as John the Baptist did when he said, "Behold, the Lamb of God" (John 1:29).

A prophet can point us toward the way, and after that it is between God and us. The prophet cannot take us to God; he can only give us the message that will guide us in the right direction.

A wise prophet gives his message from God and then gets out of the way. No prophet hangs around for the accolades of the people, because they are not coming. A prophet's job is done when he has delivered God's message.

Perhaps the greatest anguish a prophet can experience is to see the message go unheeded. It is not within the prophet's power to make the people obey God. Obedience is based upon their faith in God that brings them one step closer along the pathway to the heart of God.

*We rejoice, O God, in the message Thou hast brought to us through the faithfulness of Thy select prophets. May we humbly obey the message conveyed. In Jesus' name. Amen.*

# 4

# WHEN GOD CHOOSES A PROPHET

*And, behold, I am with thee, and will keep thee in all places whither thou goest, and will bring thee again into this land; for I will not leave thee, until I have done that which I have spoken to thee of.*

GENESIS 28:15

I t is rather interesting to read the biographies of some of the great men and women of God. Most of them, if not all, rose out of obscurity and were placed in a position of being used by God. Some of those great saints who were chosen of God would be overlooked by any church board today.

Thankfully, God sees what we cannot see and He never asks for our recommendations. When He chooses a prophet, He does so for reasons all His own.

## An Unlikely Candidate

So much could be said of that colorful man, Jacob, that it probably deserves a book of its own. You can read his story in the book of Genesis, but I want to search out the one central factor of his life that is important to us now. That important aspect of Jacob's life was that he met God in a way that utterly transformed him.

Every move of God in an individual heart begins with a deep sense of discontent. This was true of Jacob.

To begin with, Jacob was anything but a worthy character. In the first place, his home life was unfortunate. The home that the brothers, Jacob and Esau, grew up in was not ideal in any aspect. Rebekah and Isaac, their mother and father, seemingly led separate lives, though they never divorced. Rebekah favored Jacob, and Isaac favored Esau. They lived together and raised their two sons together. The neighbors never knew anything much was wrong with them, but the fact is, they were divided in their hearts.

It would be laughable if it were not so tragic that Isaac loved Esau because Esau brought home his favorite meat. Isaac loved the man Esau because Esau was a hunter and would go out and get venison for him. That is a poor excuse of a relationship between a father and son.

Rebekah's relationship with Jacob was just as toxic.

Jacob's character showed weaknesses—moral flaws that were beyond the normal. My grandmother would have said he was attached to his mother's apron string. Jacob stayed with his mother even until he was into middle life.

A major flaw with Jacob was his sneaky nature, which bordered on the perilous. Everybody he encountered he tricked into doing something. Nothing seemed to be beneath him. He was such a crook. His name, Jacob, means "crooked," so they certainly named that boy well.

Jacob had a streak of avarice in him—a streak of larceny, if you ask me. Remember the time when Jacob was cooking up some pottage, and Esau came from the field without having caught anything that day, and he was hungry? Esau was so hungry that he said to his brother, "Give me a bowl of your stew."

Jacob took advantage of the situation and said, "What will you give me?"

"I am ready to die. What is my birthright worth then?" said Esau.

"Give me your birthright and I'll give you some stew," demanded Jacob.

Jacob cheated his brother out of that birthright.

Later on, with his mother's help, Jacob cheated his father. It was a sneaking, deceitful, dirty trick that Jacob pulled on his blind father. What is confusing is that Isaac did not know his own son. He lived with those boys, yet he did not recognize their voices. He did say, "It does sound like Jacob's voice, but I will admit those are the hairy arms of Esau."

He stretched out his arms and blessed Jacob with the firstborn's blessing and never stopped to inquire of God. He seemed to do it all on his own. That is the kind of home Jacob came out of.

Jacob had a calculating, bargaining spirit; and even when he had this great vision, he brought this bargaining spirit over to his relationship with God. His attitude was, "God, if You will bless me, I will tithe."

The only thing Jacob could do morally, as far as any hope of God was concerned, was to go back and sit down. Granted, his family life was tough, his quality of character was bad and his parents showed favoritism and partiality, thus dividing the family. Jacob would have been voted the man least likely to get right with God, because there was nothing in him to recommend it.

Anybody who watched Jacob's slithery, sinuous, serpentine conduct would have said, "There's no use looking at that fellow; he is hopeless." But God saw otherwise.

There is a deep mystery here that I do not claim to understand. Somebody who may have all the characteristics of a gentleman may be a million miles from God and remain perfectly satisfied with himself. And somebody with no qualifying characteristics may be just the one God uses.

Nobody would have given any hope for Jacob to be used of God. But I have discovered that God specializes in hopeless cases.

If it were up to me, I never would have chosen Jacob. My choice would have been Esau. I find him to be a much better person than Jacob ever was. There was not really that much bad about Esau; it was always Jacob who had a crooked view of everything around him. I think I could have gotten along with Esau.

I'm thankful that it was not up to me, but up to God. God saw something in Jacob that was not in Esau. God saw in Jacob that which could be used for His purposes. Although Esau was a wonderful person, there was not anything in him that God could identify with at this point.

What was the difference?

## A Holy Discontentment

Jacob had a great dissatisfaction and discontentment with himself and a longing after God deep within. God cannot help anyone who does not first have a deep discontentment with himself. Jacob was deep in sin, but not so deep that it followed him to the life of another world. Esau was not so deep in sin, but he was satisfied with what he had. The worst thing that can be said about Esau was that he was spiritually satisfied, and that damned him.

I am not too worried about how far a man has gone, but I am greatly concerned about what direction he is headed. I am concerned whether he is aimed in the right way or not and I am concerned about whether he is longing after God. If we do not long after God, we will remain right where we are. We will come to a place where we are spiritually stalled.

Why is it that some good people are satisfied with the status quo, especially in their spiritual life? They are nice people, nice to live around, but they never have that spark. And why do some of the most crooked people, the most sinful people, with a bad disposition and evil temperament reveal that they are deeply troubled and have a longing, a spark leaping up, after God? Such was the case with Jacob.

The discontentment was God trying to get through to the man Jacob. Jacob was self-stricken because he had cheated his father; he was sick because he had to leave his mother and his home; and he was feeling afraid and uncertain and was in a state of complete loneliness. It was the perfect set-up for life transformation.

## The Path to Life Transformation

We see Jacob at his worst, but we find him on his way to meet God and become the best. Jacob the worst became Jacob the best, and Jacob the crook become a prince with God and had his name changed to Israel. What was the path that brought this change?

## Alone with God

Jacob was alone with God. You must have God all by yourself. You and God alone have to figure things out. If you have never learned or never experienced the depths of loneliness before God, chances are you are not in the position to have God do very much for you. All the great men had to go to God alone. God had to let this all work out to get Jacob by himself in a state of complete loneliness. That was when God appeared to Jacob.

Before any man will start to woo God, God must begin to woo the man. God must be there first. So God appeared to Jacob, and that was the reason for his discontent and unrest in his heart and the aimless activity he was going through. The eternal mystery had been overshadowing the man Jacob.

As Jacob fled from his home, one of the most wonderful things happened to him. He lay down that night in the wilderness, and as he slept, he saw a ladder that reached up into the heavens "and behold the angels of God ascending and descending on it" (Gen. 28:12).

## Awakened to His Need for God

The thing I like about this is that when Jacob awoke from that dream, he said, "Surely the Lord is in this place; and I knew it not" (Gen. 28:16). God was there all the time. He had been there all the time and was patiently waiting for Jacob.

Jacob awoke out of his sleep and suddenly had an awakening of the inner life. He was awakened to the shining wonder of God and His kingdom. "God is here and I knew it not" is the theme of those who have been awakened to the reality of God; who have been awakened to the fact that we belong to God, and God belongs to us; that we are His, He is ours and we do not belong to anybody else.

We need to be awakened to the fact that we must deal with God who has been following us all this time. This is the mystery, because how can it be that God comes, follows us and introduces this desire into our hearts? I just know that there is something in us akin to God. That does not mean we are saved, because "except ye repent and are born again ye shall likewise perish." Something in us responds to that Majesty we call God.

God is trying to get the signal through to us, but the ones who are satisfied with what they have hear nothing. Only those like Jacob, who are discontent and uneasy and living with a bad conscience, see something; they hear something, and they will meet God after all.

Christ is the point where we experience God. Christ is the One who is the man side of God where we can relate to God and come into fellowship with God. God is pursuing us through the Lord Jesus Christ. He wants us to break through into a state of spiritual awareness.

When Jacob awakened out of his sleep, it was more than waking out of physical somnolence; it was a sudden awakening to the shining wonder of the knowledge of God and the faith of Christ, even before His incarnation in the womb of the Virgin Mary. We can never comprehend this, nor is it something that can be explained.

We have tried to make God in our image, and because we have made Him in our image, we think we can explain everything

He is supposed to do. If you can explain everything about God, it really isn't God.

Those men who met God had spiritual experiences nobody could define, much less define it themselves. All they could do was stand in silent adoration. All they could do was rejoice. All they could do was enjoy it and thank God and obey God and come back for more and rejoice some more and go obey God some more.

**A Desire to Know God Above All Else**

As crooked as old Jacob was, he had one redeeming quality: He had a holy discontent in the depths of his heart where he wanted to know God, and God knew it. God knew that nothing could keep Jacob out if he wanted to know God bad enough, and Jacob did.

If you are not discontented, but you are satisfied with where you are, then I do not know anything that can be done. I do not know anything anybody can do. There was nothing anybody could do for Esau. Esau was satisfied with himself and his life. He possessed no spiritual longing. Nowhere in the whole life of Esau was there any evidence of moral discontent or spiritual yearning. It is the most precious treasure you have—that spiritual longing in your heart for God.

Jacob was not a prophet in the sense of what we are talking about here. Jacob illustrates for us how God can take a man who looks like nothing and can use him. God can take such a man who is discontent with his spiritual life and has a longing for God, and God can meet that man in the splendor of experience and use that man for His honor and glory. In order to be a voice for God, the prophet had to have such an encounter with God that lifted him above his own moral weakness.

*O God of Jacob, how we identify with that man, and how we identify with the discontent he experienced in his own life. May we never be satisfied with ourselves and where we are, and may we have a longing for You that will enable You to break through and meet us where we are. Amen and amen.*

# 5

# How God Prepares His Prophet

*And Jacob was left alone; and there wrestled a man with him until the breaking of the day. And when he saw that he prevailed not against him, he touched the hollow of his side; and the hollow of Jacob's thigh was out of joint, as he wrestled with him.*

GENESIS 32:24-25

In reading the story of Jacob, I find a troubling degree of deception and dishonesty and lying and intrigue and treachery. All of it is woven into Jacob's story. Everybody in the family was guilty except old Isaac. And brother Esau was a better man than Jacob was.

Jacob had committed a great wrong against his brother Esau. He first wiggled around to catch Esau when he was hungry. Jacob knew Esau lived for his stomach, so he waited for the right moment and then brewed up a mess of good stew. The aroma would make any man hungry, and when Esau arrived hungry, Jacob took the advantage and said, "Sell me your birthright and you can have the stew."

Even Jacob's own mother, Rebekah, led him down the road of treachery and deception in deceiving her husband to bless Jacob in place of Esau.

When I read this story, I do not really like Jacob very much. I think his brother was a much finer man. I think I could get along with Esau, but I would have had trouble with Jacob.

Yet, Jacob serves as a model of how God prepares His prophet. His story is the story of how a man who was not good by nature was delivered by God from the hand of a man who was not any good by grace. Jacob was delivered from out of the hand of Esau in a way he never dreamed possible.

In order for God's prophet to carry God's message to God's people, he must be uniquely prepared and qualified, and he must be delivered out of the hand of his Esau. The astonishing thing to me is that when God chooses His prophets, He does not disqualify a man because of his history. The message here is that God can take any man who will yield to Him and make him into a man He can use. It is not so much the man as it is the God who makes the man.

Dr. A. B. Simpson founded Nyack College, but Nyack College never produced an A. B. Simpson. D. L. Moody founded Moody Bible Institute, but Moody Bible Institute never produced a D. L. Moody.

Both colleges produced a great many servants of the Lord Jesus Christ. What I am getting at is simply this: Only God can prepare a prophet to do the ministry of a prophet. The schools of the prophet never produced an Elijah or an Elisha.

I believe that God takes great delight in selecting the most inconspicuous man and turning him into a prophet He can mightily use in delivering His message to His people.

Jacob was such a person. If I had to choose between Jacob and Esau, I would make the mistake of choosing Esau. The reason is that I do not see things as God sees and, therefore, I overlook what only God can see.

# Preparation to Become God's Prophet

Let me use the example of Jacob as the way God prepares a prophet for His ministry.

### He Had to Face the Past

The first thing God did with Jacob was to bring him to that point to cross over the river Jabbok to meet his yesterday. As far as Jacob was concerned, there was quite a bit of unfinished business in his past.

God will not use a man until he has closed the account on the past. When the past is closed, God brings His prophet to the point of going forward.

As long as the past beckons us for any reason, it is impossible to go forward and quite difficult to be used by God. The past cannot be ignored. Jesus died on the cross to deal with all of our past. Before God will use a man, He has to bring his accounts up to date based on what happened on that cross.

Jacob had unfinished business concerning his brother Esau. There was nobody Jacob wanted to see less than Esau, but in God's design it had to take place. Jacob had to wade across the river to meet his yesterday whether he liked it or not. Jacob had to wade across the river knowing that there was a sworn foe on the other side to fight against. The same is true for us. We have to wade across our river Jabbok whether we like it or not.

### He Had to Get Spiritually Prepared

Jacob was to learn that the way God conquers our enemies is to conquer us. It doesn't make sense from the human standpoint. But this is the vital spiritual preparation. If God could not humble Jacob completely, then Jacob could never have presented the meek and lowly aspect he did to his brother Esau. If he had met Esau with his chin out and his knuckles white, he would have been a dead man in short order. He had it coming, and all of history would have said, "I'm on Esau's side." Esau had waited years to get even with Jacob, and nobody could blame him for that.

God knew it, Jacob knew it, Esau knew it. I do not know whether Jacob told his wives about his past, but if he did, they were on their brother-in-law's side rather than Jacob's. Jacob was in a jam here; he was greatly afraid and had a right to be.

God's priority was to prepare Jacob spiritually if he was ever going to get out of the hand of Esau. So God forced Jacob to get ready.

All of your tomorrows will be of your own making. Not all of your tomorrows will be your yesterdays projected forward, but there will be some of your yesterdays in your tomorrows. You may be sure of that; and when you meet your tomorrows, whatever they may be, you have to be prepared. It is here that God uniquely prepares the man He is about to use.

Many people believe that preparation is in the areas of education and economics. Jacob had both, and yet he was highly unprepared for what God had in store for him.

Secular preparation does not prepare for the spiritually dynamic ministry entrusted to a prophet.

Spiritual preparation has nothing to do with time. Spiritual preparation is always in the hands of God. Our responsibility is obedience. Moses spent 40 years in the desert before God gave him his assignment; and Paul spent his share of time in the desert before God could use him.

### He Had to Leave the Battle Outcome to God

The third aspect of consideration in God's preparation of His prophet is that the outcome was decided before the event. No battle is ever won on the day it is fought.

Sun-tzu (544 B.C.), in his book *The Art of War,* made a very wonderful observation: "Every battle is won long before it is ever fought." All military strategists have used this advice to prepare for the battles they engage in. History shows that no battle is ever won the day it is fought, and no battle is ever lost the day it is fought.

King Saul died on Gilboa, but he lost at Endor when he consulted the witch to call up Samuel, who told him he would be dead before morning.

What you do today has great bearing upon tomorrow. Tomorrow's battles are won or also lost today.

### He Had to Get to the Root of the Problem

Another important aspect of a prophet's preparation is also seen in Jacob. To get out of Esau's hands, Jacob had to learn that all life, at its root, is spiritual. Therefore, all problems are solved only by a spiritual solution. This is a difficult lesson for us to learn. _Submission to the Will of God_

We have been taught otherwise. We are given solutions that are psychological, educational, intellectual and even economical. These solutions only deal with surface issues. You can deal with a man's financial problems and yet at the core of that man is a problem that finances will never touch.

In order for Jacob to get out of Esau's hands, he could not stand up to him nose to nose. Esau would have whipped him in nothing flat. Jacob was no match, physically, for Esau. Esau had everything on his side.

Jacob had to learn that at the core of his problem was a spiritual problem that could only be remedied by a spiritual solution. Jacob wrestled all night with God before he submitted to this truth. God had to conquer Jacob before Jacob could ever conquer Esau. This is always God's way.

The solution to all of our problems is spiritual. All real dangers are spiritual dangers, and there is not any other kind. Jesus warned, "And fear not them which kill the body, but are not able to kill the soul: but rather fear him which is able to destroy both soul and body in hell" (Matt. 10:28). Jesus said that our problem is a spiritual danger, not a physical danger, and our visible enemies are rarely our real enemies. The man who comes at you with a gun is not your real enemy, though his intention may be to kill you. Your real enemy is that within you which makes you vulnerable to him.

Esau was Jacob's enemy because of what Jacob had done to him, but Esau was not Jacob's real enemy. Jacob was Jacob's enemy. The crookedness in Jacob's heart was against Jacob, and when God straightened that out, Esau was not his enemy anymore.

The source of our real danger is spiritual, and if we will get our inward life fixed up, our outward enemies will be helpless.

When the devil came around to Jesus, Jesus said of him, "For the prince of this world cometh, and hath nothing in me" (John 14:30). The devil can only get in you if he has something in there that belongs to him. If he does not have anything in there that belongs to him, he can only go around the outside and growl. He cannot get in. All problems have their spiritual solution. As we become adjusted to the will of God, we win; but if we are not adjusted to the will of God, we lose. It is as simple as that.

## He Had to Let God Conquer Him

Another lesson from Jacob's life in the way God prepares a man for ministry is that if God conquers a man, he is unconquerable.

Jacob was a sorry figure in those early years; he was scheming, calculating, bargaining, lying, fleeing, deceiving, cheating and being cheated, and the list goes on and on. Then God came along, broke the strength of Jacob and made him into Israel because he had prevailed. When God conquered Jacob, he lived and died a prince in Israel.

God conquers our foes by conquering us. This is the hardest preparation for us to take. But remember that God always conquers your enemy by conquering you. God never fights on the side of the man who holds his fist clenched. If you are going out there to knock the block off that fellow, God will simply let you knock it off. If you cannot, the probability or even possibility is that your block will suffer in the process. God is not fighting on the side of the man who is out to knock another man's block off.

If you come to yourself and allow God to do His work in your life, He brings you to the point of being conquered and, therefore, nobody else can conquer you.

We do not like it this way. We like God to come to our side and we pray, "O God, come and make me victorious." God, however, does not answer this prayer, nor does He work this way. God will come and conquer you and then the enemy has no power over you.

Many years ago, God gave me Exodus 23 in a special way. I think it has almost become my life chapter. When He gave me that, He told me that He would make my enemies turn their backs on me. I have believed from that hour until this that the only part of my enemy that I have any right to seize is the back of his neck. My enemy cannot bother me as long as I keep myself under the hand of God. When I render up my sword, then I am victorious. As long as I hold it, I lose. That is when I am fighting in my own strength. Fire cannot burn twice over the same place, and neither can a conquest of God burn twice over the same place. He moves in on your soul and humbles you beneath Him. After that, He will ensure that nobody else can do it.

### He Had to Become Humble

Jacob's story also illustrates the final stage of training. Jacob learned when he got out of the hand of Esau that humility wins where force can never win. If Jacob had taken a weapon, he would have had to rely upon that weapon. He would have faced Esau on Esau's terms and would have lost the battle. Humility always wins where force cannot win.

Jacob won by surrendering first to God and then to Esau. Jacob appears very well in humble dress. He appears better in humble dress than he did in the bold dress of his former days. Do not think that it is a sign of weakness to be humble; it is a sign of strength. It is a sign of weakness when we become arrogant and proud. It is not degrading at all for us to take the lowly place.

A man came to a Welsh preacher and confessed that he was having trouble at home. The Welsh preacher summed it up pretty well and advised this man, "I don't know your home and I don't know you and I don't know your wife. I only know one side of your story, but I do know one thing. When there is trouble in the home, almost always humility will take care of it."

If one side or the other will humble himself, it will take care of the problem. It is somewhat hard to hold a fight all by yourself; so if only one side is fighting, the fight will die out for want of fuel.

When we are compelled to cross our Jabbok, some of those crossings will be of our own making, and we might as well admit it. I have gone over a few times and faced up to some fellows that I did not like to face up to but had to. We all have to do this. And some of those crossings will not be of our own making, but we will be carrying the cross for Christ. The frightening part about it all is that our loved ones are in danger along with us. The best protection your family can have is a humble father. God will not allow anyone to destroy a humble house. He will not permit an enemy to come in and destroy a house where the head of the family is humble before God. God puts an umbrella over such a home.

I do not say that God might not allow sickness to occur. I do not say that He might not in His sovereign wisdom take some of them home. I do say there will be no injury done. There is a difference between being hurt and being injured.

There is a difference between having real harm done to you and merely being bruised a bit. In the good will of God, He lets His children get bruised, but nothing finally can hurt them. You cannot hurt a good man.

If we go down in complete surrender, we take a shortcut to victory. If we stand up and fight for ourselves, we take a shortcut to defeat. Our God loves doing such things on our part. He loves it when we humble ourselves.

We get out of the hand of Esau by learning that spiritual preparation is vital, and the outcome is not decided the day the battles are fought, but back through the years in our spiritual relationship with God. In addition, a God-conquered man cannot be conquered by anything else, and humility wins where force cannot possibly win. God take seriously the man who takes God seriously.

*Eternal God, take us over our Jabbok and lead us to victory by conquering us. May our victory be Your victory. Amen.*

# 6

# GETTING THE PROPHET'S ATTENTION

*And when Abram was ninety years old and nine,*
*the LORD appeared to Abram, and said unto him, I am the*
*Almighty God; walk before me, and be thou perfect.*

GENESIS 17:1

I hesitate to talk about this, for I feel unworthy, because here is found the beating heart of living religion. Abram had no Bible, no church, no religious conviction, no Bible teacher, no evangelist, no hymnal, no Bible school. He only had his empty, hungry heart and God. Here we see the ancient fountain of worship. This goes back to the roots of true religion from which have sprung all denominations, all churches, all forms of worship, all those things we take for granted—organs and pianos and seers and preachers. Abram had none of those things.

Abram was a man who met God.

Father Abraham stands for every man, and he is the father of all those who believe. He had no religious problems; or if he did, he took them straight to God. He talked to God.

(How many people are in hell today because they fooled them-selves into thinking they had a religious problem when it was a sin problem, and they had no desire to be rid of it.)

Abram met God in a living encounter. Notice that God stepped over the threshold into Abram's experience, into his cognitive experience. God met Abram face to face.

With every man of God, especially the prophet, it all begins by consciously being aware of God. This is the starting point. It begins with a divine encounter where God steps across the threshold into our experience.

That's what happened to Abram. The living, vibrant, audi-ble Word of the Lord came to Abram.

## Divine Encounter

I firmly believe in spiritual experiences. This goes all the way back to the early Christian church, to the apostles and even to our Lord Jesus Christ Himself. These all had experiences with God that confirmed the Word of God.

The trouble with us today is that we believe without confir-mation. We do not have God's Word confirmed in our hearts. God does not need to confirm anything in Himself, because God, being true, cannot lie; but we need confirmation in our-selves. If we do not get it, we are very poor, anemic, disappointed and dissatisfied Christians. By definition, this confirmation ex-perience starts with conscious awareness. To be aware of some-thing . . . that cannot be broken down any further. You are aware of something and then you become consciously aware of it.

Looking at Abram, the question that comes to mind is, what was he consciously aware of? We have here the fact of a conscious awareness of something by somebody, and I positively defy any theologian or preacher in the world to take that away from the church of Christ. You have a right to be consciously aware of meeting God. You have a right to that confirmation—that inward knowledge, that witness within you of God. This is much more than my personal opinion. The church fathers believed this down through the years.

When God stepped over the threshold of Abram's conscious experience, this was the divine invasion into Abram's life experience. When a man meets God, there is an awareness that lifts his heart to the elements of rapture.

Notice how this encounter affected Abram.

## Facedown on the Ground

Abram fell on his face and God talked with him. I do not think you will find in the Bible a better picture of the right place for Abram and the right place for man and the right place for God than this one: God on His throne speaking, Abram on his face listening. That is always the ideal: God doing the talking and man doing the listening.

I charge that in the modern evangelical church we are not consciously aware of a Presence. We are not consciously aware of God. We do not hear God's voice; we hear only a recording of His voice. We do not see God's face; we see only a painting of His face. We hear not the sound of His voice; we hear but an echo of that sound. We are always once removed from God.

When we stop looking at a picture of God and begin looking at God; when we stop hearing the echo and hear God's voice itself; when instead of having God in history we have Him in experience, we will begin to know what Abram knew when he fell on his face before God.

Today the church is satisfied with the God of history, with the Christ of history. We have God in history and Christ in history, but we do not have God in living personal experience. This is why we are so dissatisfied and so empty and have so little vibrant joy in the things of God.

The man Abram lay facedown in the conscious presence of that awful, overwhelming mystery that someone called the *mysterium tremendum*. He fell to his face before this awful One who was present and pressing in on him and rising above him and defeating him and taking away his self-confidence and overwhelming him. Yet, the Presence was also inviting him and calling him and pleading with him, promising him and drawing him near to God. This is God my beloved.

In our day, we have reduced God to where we can get hold of Him, manage Him and push Him around. In reality the great God and Father of our Lord Jesus Christ rises above our consciousness and above our ability to lay hold and rises beyond all of our questions into His infinitude— the mighty great God.

This is the God who approached Abram.

If we live and buy and sell and prosper, and we eat and sleep and marry and propagate, and get old and die, and we never, during all this time, meet the God of Abraham—the *mysterium tremendum*, the awful Majesty that sits upon the throne—what have we done? How are we better off than the sheep out in the pastures if we never see this . . . if heaven is silent and the night unpopulated?

## Take the World, But Give Me Jesus
### Fanny Crosby (1820–1915)

Take the world, but give me Jesus,
All its joys are but a name;
But His love abideth ever,
Through eternal years the same.

Refrain:

Oh, the height and depth of mercy!
Oh, the length and breadth of love!
Oh, the fullness of redemption,
Pledge of endless life above!

As for me, I have grown rather sick of this world and all of the pleasures it offers. They are temporary and usually go away as quickly as they come. The world tries to misdirect me from my ultimate destination, which is in heaven. We find ourselves running here and there, getting the toys and comforts of this world only to find them unsatisfying to the inner soul. I agree with the songwriter, "Take the world, but give me Jesus," for He is the only thing that truly satisfies both now and eternally.

Jesus asked, "For what is a man profited, if he shall gain the whole world, and lose his own soul? or what shall a man give in exchange for his soul?" (Matt. 16:26). This question needs to be asked by everyone and the answer will reveal a lot about that person. What are you willing to give in exchange for your soul?

A. W. TOZER

Abram got hold of an idea, just one good idea. It was simply this: *Only God matters.*

The divine purpose of God is to reveal Himself to man in conscious awareness. Abraham, the man, met God in such a manner that nothing else really mattered. Once he reveled in the presence of God, nothing else really satiated his heart. I think I can honestly say that Abram became obsessed with God.

What is desperately needed in the church today are men and women who are so obsessed with God that only God matters. I am tired of the toys and the jingle-bell-boys and all of the entertainment from the world being siphoned into the church to try to entertain the church. If we can be entertained, then we have not truly experienced the conscious presence of God. We have not met the *mysterium tremendum* that will separate us from all other appetites and will give us such an obsession for God that only God matters.

Everything has a design and a purpose, and yet it can be converted to another purpose. We see this too often today. Your ear, for example, is best when it is doing the thing God designed it to do: hear. Your ears can also be used to hang your glasses on. That, however, is not what God designed them to do.

## Facedown and Listening to the Divine

Here is what God was saying to Abram: "I am trying to get a message through to you. I am trying to tell you something; and if you listen to Me, here it is. Abram, you were made in My image; you were designed for one purpose, and that is to be a retainer at my court and a worshiper at my throne. You are to glorify Me and live in My presence and rest neither day nor night throughout eternity, crying, 'Holy, holy, holy, Lord God Almighty,' and be happy beyond the power of all mortals to understand. That is what I created you for, Abram. Don't forget it." I do not think Abram ever did.

Abram finally modeled the reason that we have been created. We are first of all to be worshipers—that is what God created you for. God put a harp in your soul, and He is the only one who can get any music out of the harp. God put that harp there, God put that image of Himself there so that you might take it to Him and He might use it and play on that instrument and bring forth music to fill all the heavens above. Abram had to learn to glorify God. That is what we need to learn too. Nothing else really matters.

Only God matters, at last; and if you get everything settled with God and get God within the compass of your spiritual experience, He will untangle everything else.

All problems at the very core are spiritual; and if you get God, everything else will align itself. But it does not make much difference whether things align or not, for you do not have a long time to stay around. Awareness will lead to divine hearing. To believe in God and never hear God is what religion is all about. It is not enough to have the passive belief that there must be a God somewhere. It was not enough for Abram, and it is not enough for us today. God wants to create a divine awareness in us so that we can see and hear the voice of God.

In order for that to happen, we must be detached from all outside interference. As it was in the case of Abram, and all the other prophets throughout the Scripture, so it will be with us. God will go to any length to free us from any outside interferences. Whatever it takes to bring us to that point, as Abram was brought, God is willing to do because of His great desire for our fellowship.

The Lord appeared unto Abram, and there Abram built an altar unto the Lord.

### Spirit of God, Descend upon My Heart
George Croly (1780–1860)

Teach me to love Thee as Thine angels love,
One holy passion filling all my frame;
The kindling of the heaven descended Dove,
My heart an altar, and Thy love the flame.

God had been there all the time. But Abram had just become acquainted with Him, and this has been true for every worshiper. All the great souls, all the great saints from the highest born to the lowest born, from kings to peasants, tell the same thing. When they met the great God Almighty, something changed them, something changed inside of them, and the complexion and color of the universe changed for them.

### I Am His, and He Is Mine
George W. Robinson (1838–1877)

Heav'n above is softer blue,
Earth around is sweeter green!
Something lives in every hue

Christless eyes have never seen;
Birds with gladder songs o'erflow,
flowers with deeper beauties shine,
Since I know, as now I know,
I am His, and He is mine.
Since I know, as now I know,
I am His, and He is mine.

Everything looks good when God is in your heart. Everything looks good when seen through the glow of worship and the aura of divine enjoyment.

That is the picture we get of Abram in Genesis 17. We get a picture of that mysterious Presence—that fire, that great darkness, that awesome thing we read about there. Here was experience in mystery and majesty and awe and wonder. That feeling of personal nothingness came upon the man Abram before that object we call God. Abram was bewildered, confused, captivated, transported, ravished and fascinated. All this came to the heart of the man. This is what made Abram become Abraham.

## And Abraham Worshiped

We do not build physical altars today, but for us an altar is a sacred area. It is the place where only God matters. It is the place where we are separated from everything else—all noise, all chatter. It is a place where we are consecrated for one purpose, and that is to worship God.

Only the separated man will hear with clarity the voice of God. The separation must be from all voices and noises without. All other voices are to be put aside so that the voice of God can be clearly heard by the man of God.

In order for God to use a man, he has to be separated so that God can speak to him in such a way that the man can hear God. Only the man who can hear God can speak for God.

There is a danger today of not hearing clearly, to hear only a partial voice, a garbled voice, and not get the message clear. This is the great peril we find ourselves in today among the evangelical church.

The danger lies in the area of thinking something is right when it is not. To go through the motions does not make it a reality. The reality only comes when God is able to invade a person and step across the threshold of conscious awareness. The reality comes when the written Word becomes a Living Word, and we hear distinctly the voice of God.

This is the danger of hearing partial truth. This is what makes heretics. It is not that they are not telling some aspect of the truth. I find that even among evangelical churches there is only partial truth being expounded. The reason is because someone is only hearing the partial voice of God. He is hearing a voice from a distance, an echo that cannot be clearly distinguished. Because, you see, the part you do not hear can destroy.

## Majesty Divine
### Frederick W. Faber (1814–1863)

O Blessed Trinity!
In the deep darkness of prayer's stillest night
We worship Thee blinded with light.

Holy Trinity!
Blessed Equal Three,
One God, we praise Thee.
O Blessed Trinity!
Oh, would that we could die of love for Thee,
Incomparable Trinity!
Holy Trinity!
Blessed Equal Three,
One God, we praise Thee.

Our fathers had this flame. But where is that living flame that has shone so brightly in the days of old? We do not have it because we have not experienced it. We have come in by saying, "I accept Christ." We signed the card; we joined something, but we have not really met God.

*O living God, break through the hard shell of our personality and invade us so that we might become consciously aware of Thy blessed presence. This I pray, in Jesus' name. Amen.*

# 7

# THE SECRET OF THE PROPHET'S SUCCESS

*And the woman said to Elijah, Now by this I know that thou art a man of God, and that the word of the LORD in thy mouth is truth.*

1 KINGS 17:24

I do not hesitate to call Elijah a saint. Although he was a man, of like passion, he was still a man after God's heart. This man, though among the very greatest of the Old Testament or, indeed, the greatest of Bible heroes, was a man who had almost nothing to recommend him.

If Elijah were to turn up some Sunday morning, we probably would not let him in the church; or if we did, we certainly would not let him in the pulpit. Although this man lacked so many desirable qualities and had so many undesirable qualities, there was something about him that God honored and blessed. The most wonderful thing of all is that God let him stand as a beacon light on top of a hill for all the ages that followed to get light and encouragement.

What was the secret of this man Elijah? What did he have or didn't have, or what position or attitude did he take? What was it about him that God could use? How was it that Elijah had courage to stand against the false prophets?

## After Standing in God's Presence

The secret of Elijah's courage was that he had been with God and stood in His presence. He had discovered the ultimate reality. Very few people come to this point of ultimate reality. To stand in God's presence is to prepare a man to stand before anybody else without fear. Here was a man who found something that lasted.

We miss the ultimate reality today because of sin; and yet, man is always striving after it. What is it that stirs up people to do crazy things? It is that which is of God within them fighting with that which is of sin within them, and consequently, they do not act natural. The great hymn writer Philip Doddridge put it this way: "Now rest, my long-divided heart, fixed on this blissful center, rest." Edward Mote underscored these words with the hymn lyrics, "I dare not trust the sweetest frame but wholly lean on Jesus' name."

When Elijah found the holy in the midst of the impure, he found the absolute and ultimate reality. He found the infinite beyond the limited. Elijah found the perfect in the midst of the imperfect. He also found the eternal within the temporal.

Elijah found all of this; and what he had found was not a philosophy. Many religious people are just religious philosophers, and they are not very good ones at that. They get wild and spend a lifetime promulgating their religious philosophy. Elijah did not find a religious philosophy; Elijah found God. Elijah did not find a religion or key of life. Elijah found God, and there is a world of difference between finding these things and finding God.

You can be baptized and take Communion, and you can yield to and formulate your life after all of the ways of the church, and yet be empty and miserable, because God made us for Himself, and our hearts are dissatisfied until we find our satisfaction in God. It is God that we need. It is God that we lost when we sinned; it is God that we get back when we are saved; and it is God that we miss and need. Elijah found God.

Elijah found, as his ancestor Abram had found, that only God matters. He said to the great King, "I stand before God."

In following Elijah's life, we see that this man's spiritual encounter was tested in the fire of living. There is a great breakdown in modern Christianity. We take things at secondhand, we have never had a true encounter with God and we cannot relate our religion to our lives. Some people's religion goes east while they are going west. They go in one direction and their religion goes in another, and the twain shall never meet.

## Tested in the Fire of Living

The secret of the prophet is also the secret of victorious Christian living today. If we are going to have the courage to break through and discover ultimate reality, we need to discover God in the midst of our life.

What did you do last week differently than you would have done if you had not been a Christian? How do you live differently every day?

We talk about love, but how much did you spend on yourself and how much did you give away? We talk about sacrifice, but did you sacrifice riding in a big car, sleeping on a beauty rest mattress and eating three times a day? Any sacrifice? What are we doing that we would not be doing if we were not Christians? What is the difference? I would like to know that there is a difference.

Is Jesus Christ simply the boutonniere on the human lapel—something nice, something pretty? Is Christianity just a decoration, or is there reality back of it?

Elijah discovered the reality. He found it, and his spiritual life was tested in the fire of living. He related his faith to his works, his beliefs to his life. Much of Christianity in our time is simply a lovely symbol; there is no living reality back of it.

A man is supposed to be a Christian, but push him enough and he goes to pieces. Many Christians live a Christian life: they are born again, carry the Bible translation du jour, attend Bible conferences and are a part of the religious life of their day. But when the pressure is on, religion goes one way and they go another.

## Belief Takes Flesh

Elijah was not guilty of that. Elijah had seen God and been with God, and his religious notions did not vanish under pressure. He stood up because he had been with God. "I am

Elijah; I stand before God." Everything he believed had been tested in the fire experience.

Elijah was a man of courage, and it became incarnated in him. I believe that God wants to incarnate the Word again in human life. We need that more than we need anything else. We are to become the incarnated Word, walking around giving flesh to the doctrines we believe. If this would happen, we would have on our hands such a surge of Christian work and testimony never known before in this generation.

God gave us Elijah that we might see a man who was the incarnation of what he believed. You could not separate him from what he believed.

It is easy to separate some people from their religion. A man comes home Sunday night, takes his religion off, hangs it in the closet and does not put it on until the next Sunday morning. You could not separate Elijah from his religion. You could see him in any direction and you were always running into his faith, because the man was a man of faith all the way through.

In my opinion, the reason some preachers do not get anywhere is that they are never willing to enlarge the area of their vulnerability. They always attempt to keep themselves protected; but even a mud turtle cannot get anywhere until he sticks his neck out. As long as he holds his neck in, he just lies there and looks dumb. But as soon as he sticks his neck out, then come the legs and the tail, and he gets going.

Elijah was a man who was not afraid to stick his neck out. I would have loved to meet Elijah, and I hope to someday. He will not be as rough there, I am sure. He will not have those garments. He will have different garments on. He will be more approachable than he was in that day.

In looking at all of these prophets, especially Elijah, we can see that they were notoriously hard to live with. Here was a man who let his faith in God cost him something. He did not go to church once a week and give an occasional donation. His was a deep and serious descent from the popular world of his day—the world of Jezebel and Ahab, and Baal, and the rest of them. His religion was a deep, radical, grave, treasonable descent; it was treasonable, because he stood against a king, albeit a wicked king. He received a commission from God to stand against the world, and he stood alone. "I only, I only."

Elijah's religious notions did not vanish under pressure. This is the loneliness of serving God. The rest of the prophets, some 7,000 of them, were silent, and nobody knew they were there. That was the terrible part of it.

Where lay the power of this great man of God? He had been with God and stood in His presence; his faith was tested in the fire of living; he had the courage to stand against religious corruption. That is what made Elijah great, and it cost this man painful discipline.

Today we have fixed up Christianity so that we go around telling people how easy it is. We gather people together and say, "You've got it all wrong. Jesus is not going to lay any burdens on you. He is going to take them off. He is not going to let you get into trouble; He is going to pull you out of trouble. Serving the Lord is the easiest, smoothest, slickest thing in all the world. You can have a wonderful time and just be happy, happy, happy, and then go to heaven." Many people believe in this contorted position of being a Christian.

# A Necessary Humiliation

If we had the courage of Elijah, we would tell them, "If you will follow Jesus, you will have His enemies; if you follow Jesus, you will have His troubles; if you follow Jesus, you will have His rejection; if you follow Jesus, they will think the same of you as they did of Him, and what they thought of Him can be seen on a hill outside Jerusalem. They took Him out and nailed Him on the cross."

Elijah knew all of this. Elijah knew God, and it cost him dearly. He had to accept personal humiliation.

Remember, during the time of the drought Elijah had to go down by a little stream where the birds brought him food in the morning and he drank out of the stream. What a humiliating thing that was for a man who had been his own boss all his life and had come from a great rough country from the highlands of Gilead. Now he was sitting beside that stream, watching the ravens bring him bread.

God's prophecy, however, started coming true. There was no rain, and very soon there was not even a stream. At that point, Elijah looked like a blunder and a failure, and I can imagine that the devil came and tormented him.

When there was no stream, no rains, and Elijah was hungry and thirsty, the Lord came to him and said, "Elijah, get thee up and go into the land; the town Zarephath and there a widow woman will feed thee" (see 1 Kings 17:8-9). Imagine the compounded humiliation. It was bad enough to have a raven feed you, but now he had to have a widow woman; and the whole thing was given for the humbling of the man Elijah.

There stands this man of God, Elijah, in history. He did not try to push people around, but he did stand for what he stood for. God said, "There I put him up for you to look at. Look at him and be a better woman. Look at him and be a better man. Look at him and be a humbler person. Look at him and glorify God, for Elijah's God still lives today."

The Lord heard the voice of Elijah. Why does it say the Lord heard the voice of Elijah? Elijah was willing to hear the voice of God. If you want God to hear your voice, first you are going to have to hear God's voice. If you will not hear God's voice, and you get in a jam and scream to high heaven, and want God to hear your voice, God is not going to put Himself in your hands like that. If you are going to be heard of God, God will have to be heard of you. God heard Elijah because Elijah heard God. God did what Elijah asked because Elijah had done what God asked.

The souls of the righteous are in the hands of God, and no evil can befall them, and not all the world's charm could pull Elijah away.

This is the secret of Elijah's power, and this is the secret for us today to have power over the world around us.

## Putting On Elijah's Mantle

Who will bid for Elijah's mantle? Who will bid for Elijah's power? Who will apply for the faith of standing before God as Elijah did?

We can rule out the coward; he cannot have that job. We can rule out the self-lover, the sin-lover, the world-lover. They cannot have that job; only the fearless need apply. Only the faithful need apply; but through Jesus Christ our Lord, you can apply. All this was done under the shadow of the cross. Elijah looked forward to the cross, and we look backward to the cross; but it is the same cross. Elijah lived in the power of Christ to come, and we live in the power of Christ who came; but it is the same Christ.

The man who will hear God is the man God will hear; the man who will allow his spiritual experiences to be tested in the fire of living is the man who will dare if needed to stand against the world. God will bless that man. God will hold that man close and watch over him and love him and keep him and bless him—all by grace through mercy, but also by the conditions of obedience and faith.

Are we softened and weakened and the message stated to a place where we do not even understand these men? Anything God did for Elijah, He will do for you by way of spiritual power, blessing, warmth, faithfulness, intimacy and grace.

> *Dear God of Elijah who is the God of today, may we stand boldly in Thy presence so that we can stand against the wiles of the devil and the ways of the world. Through Jesus Christ our Lord, amen.*

# 8

# THE CHALLENGE OF
# THE PROPHET

*And call ye on the name of your gods, and I will call on the name
of the LORD: and the God that answereth by fire, let him be God.
And all the people answered and said, It is well spoken.*

1 KINGS 18:24

The one thing I have never really been able to figure
out is why those who have a religion that is right do
not believe it half the time; and those who have a
religion that is all mixed up, false, miserable and degrading
believe it fervently?

Elijah confronted such a situation.

Israel had the true religion but barely believed any of it.
On the other side was the religion of the Baalites.

We see this in Ahab and Jezebel.

Ahab was king of Israel; not much of a king really, but
he filled the place for the time being. He was a Jew and was
supposed to be a worshiper of Jehovah, but he was a Jew in

name only. His wife, Jezebel, was a worshiper of Baal. In the family, Jezebel ruled. She fanatically believed her religion.

You could not worship Baal for very long before you were worse than you were when you started because of the degrading character of the worship. It had cruel and immoral rituals.

Israel suffered a moral dilemma here. Their royal family was Ahab the Jew and his wife, Jezebel, the Baalite. Ahab was committed, at least nominally, to the worship of Jehovah, and Jezebel was committed positively to the worship of Baal. This put Israel in a state of dilemma.

Israel had the divine revelation—the Holy Scriptures—that nobody else had. Besides, they had examples of good men down through the years but it did not seem enough for them.

I cannot write a line of music, and I cannot sing on pitch, but I have this ability to enjoy music until it hurts. I believe it is possible to appreciate good people, even better people than we are. That is why I believe in reading the Scriptures constantly, in order that I might fellowship with holy men and women. If I am not that good, I can at least appreciate them as I mingle with them. There seeps into my heart by a kind of spiritual osmosis a little bit of what they are and I am a better man for having gone along with them.

So, Israel knew what was right not only by the deep knowledge in their hearts, but also by the instruction from the Scriptures, by the examples of good men and by that inner voice which is the Holy Spirit.

Israel knew what was right, knew who to worship, knew how they should live, but it happened that the popular vote went the other way. All of Israel worshiped the way Jezebel worshiped. The people were too weak and cowardly to obey God; they found it easier to follow the vogue of the day.

## True Religion, or the Religion du Jour?

Everybody needs to decide whether this religious business is of God, whether God is in this, whether the Bible is real, whether hell is hell and heaven is heaven, or whether we can simply follow the vogue and be like everybody else. We need to make up our minds along this line.

Israel was in that state. The question before Israel was, is it going to be Baal or Jehovah? Elijah challenged Israel, "How long halt ye between two opinions? If the LORD be God, follow him: but if Baal, then follow him" (1 Kings 18:21).

In the original, it says, "How long will hop you along on two unequal legs?" On Thursday, they were up on the long leg with Jehovah; but Friday they got down on the low leg that was Baal, and on Saturday they got up on the high leg, which was Jehovah again. They were trying to walk in the middle, but there was one leg shorter than the other.

This was the Baal way. After all, the religion of the day was the religion of Baal. A religion will let you get away with anything if you just talk about love and the unity of mankind and the brotherhood of the world. If you just talk nice and sound very pious, you can just about do anything. The sky is the limit. There is no morality, no righteousness or godliness required. Just live any way, provided that at last you say, "We're all going to the same place; we're just going by different roads." That sounds very spiritual, and that is the way Jezebel talked.

Her argument was that Baal had something to be said in his favor. Of course, there were the sex orgies and rites of iniquity to worship him, but that was all right. That was just their way of looking at things.

What did Baal offer? What does the world offer, and what does the chief shallow religious world offer?

They offer the customary fun and conformity. Conform and go along with the crowd. Jehovah calls you to the good, hard way with its present cost and its eternal compensations.

What has Baal to offer? What has the world to offer when we surrender to the world?

The world would lead you to believe it has a lot to offer; but how utterly helpless it is when disaster strikes. Only a Christian knows how to die. Everybody has to die, but only a Christian can die with dignity. Only a Christian can die with peace in his heart. The world makes you believe it has the answer, but the world does not have the answer. The world is a painted mask, and behind that painted mask is fear upon the faces of the men and women who march up and down. They have to have amusements, fun, liquor, dope, immoral dance and all the rest in order to keep from crying out in fright like a child in the dark. They cover up the fact that they are scared, by making a lot of racket and calling it fun, and then they pay people for it.

God calls you to be a soldier, a good, hard soldier. I never could figure out why ministers feel they have to pat and paw over everybody to get them in, why they have to dilute and edit and modify and amend and trim down the gospel. It does not work this way. A trimmed-down gospel never saved a soul. A trimmed-down, diluted, edited religion is not the religion Christ died to establish. Heaven is not filled with weaklings who had to have somebody go along and help them over the rough spots. It is full of soldiers and martyrs, and the dreamers and the prophets and the clean man who loved his God and loved his generation and lived and died living a good life—a hard life.

We have to make up our minds. Are we going to go the way the world goes?

Of course, sin has its pleasure. But you have to break with that. You have to break from it and follow Jehovah. The worse the country is, and the worse the state of society, the harder it is to break, and the more it is going to cost you to break.

The world has something to offer, all right. If you do not want to follow the Lord Jesus Christ, if Baal be God, then follow him. But if the Lord Jesus Christ be God, follow Him. See to it that you make up your mind. Do not be in the middle because you are neither hot nor cold.

## What the World Has to Offer

What does the world really have to offer? Let me just name a few.

### Entertainment

The world entices us with its offering of fun. If you are able to enjoy it, if you have health, you can have fun. If you are in an economic position so that you have time off, then you can have fun. One thing capitalism has done in this country is enable us to have time off for fun. The average person works for a short time so that he might have fun for a while. He is willing to work hard at a price for the fun that he will have later. So the world will give you fun if you want it.

But when it is all over, what then?

If Jehovah should be God, if this is true, and if Jesus Christ says, "Take up your cross and follow me," and if there is to be a judgment, and God is to try every man's heart according to his thoughts and his deeds, then what about that thing the world offered you? You had your fun. Now take your medicine. Every time you are led astray, remember that the person who led you astray leaves you in the lurch.

**Material Goods**

The world also offers you possessions. You can pile up possessions. Here in the Western world, we are rich, and we have piled up possessions as high as a mountain.

Did you ever stop to think that if you are not delivered from your possessions, they will curse you? If you get delivered from them, you can have them and lose them and it will be all right.

**Temporary Success**

The world also offers position and fame. Most of us will not make it as far as fame is concerned. The only time we get mentioned in the newspaper is when we get into the obituary section. The world offers position and fame, which is about as temporary as anything going these days.

Success is also something the world offers. The world is full of successful people, and there is always room for one more. As far as the world is concerned, success has a dollar sign to it. The more money you have, the more successful you are. I have met those successful people, and very rarely do you find one who is truly happy. They are anxious about hanging on to their success.

The world can offer you position, fame, fun, entertainment and all the rest, but what can the world do for you at the last?

## What God Offers His Followers

You want forgiveness of sins, but there is not a boxing arena in the world that can give it to you. No theater in the world can give it to you. No tavern on the continent can give it to you. You want inward cleansing, but there is not anywhere in the world where you can get it.

### Forgiveness of Sin

The world has its fun, but it cannot cleanse you on the inside. Only the blood of the Lord Jesus Christ can provide that inward cleansing that we so desire.

The world cannot offer a power to direct your life in the right way. You want someone who can guide you and lead you through. Baal cannot do it. The world cannot do it. Baal can give you a big-time Saturday night, but come Sunday morning, he leaves you with a frightful hangover.

### Guidance Through Life

The power of true religion is seen in the power it has to direct our way.

This is the day of counselors. Everybody has to be counseled; but I read in the Scriptures that His name shall be called Counselor. There is one who knows, and it is not Baal.

Elijah challenged the Baal prophets. It was the true religion challenging the false religion. He stood up against that when everybody else had faded into the background. It was one man, Elijah, against the world of Baal. This is the responsibility of the prophet of God, to challenge the false religion. God's man cannot back down. The sacred contest before Elijah demanded that he be committed utterly to the true religion of Jehovah.

Elijah knew who God was, and when he prayed, God answered. The Baal prophets prayed all day and cut themselves, but nothing happened. Elijah, confident in his standing with God, mocked them, made fun of them, which only infuriated them and caused them to work harder to get Baal's attention.

When the prophets of Baal had exhausted themselves, it was Elijah's turn. When Elijah prayed a prayer that you could read in less than 30 seconds, the fire came down. God confirmed Elijah's faith and witness to his obedience.

That is what God wants to do for us today. Let us take up Elijah's mantle, challenge all the Baal prophets of the world and demonstrate to the world the mighty power of God.

*Oh, Christ, Emmanuel—God with us—the Word made flesh to dwell among us, who has risen again and who is with us now, make us strong to take up our cross, to turn our backs upon Baal and all he stands for. Help us in this hour to make up our minds and let Christ be our God. Amen.*

# 9

# WHERE IS THE LORD GOD OF ELIJAH?

*And he took the mantle of Elijah that fell from him,*
*and smote the waters, and said, Where is the LORD God of Elijah?*
*and when he also had smitten the waters, they parted hither*
*and thither: and Elisha went over.*

2 KINGS 2:14

The church today is in a state of senility. I truly wish I did not have to talk like this. I wish I could talk about sweetness and lilacs and old lace. I need, however, to put the truth of the Word of God to the situation at hand.

## A Church in Senility

Allow me to point out some of the marks of senility.

### Inflexible

The very first sign of senility is stiffness. That ability to stoop down quickly and scoop up something that fell on the floor leaves you when you are about middle age; so you do not move as quickly anymore. You move in straight lines because you no longer have the limberness you used to have. Stiffness also gets into our thinking. We think in straight lines, and it is very hard to get us to think of anything new.

A new church can think of new things, but a church that has been around a long while has a difficult time doing anything that was not done before. They continue to do something expensive and useless for 25 years. Nobody dares to question that. They are stiff. It is a sign of old age.

## All Talk and No Action
Another sign of old age is loquacity, which is the tendency to talk an awful lot. The older the church gets, the more she talks. Anything can be cured, any problem solved, if you just talk long enough. If anything goes wrong, meet and have a talkfest; and when it is all over, everybody goes home, nothing has been helped, but there have been many words thrown around.

## Weakness and Lack of Movement
Weakness is another mark of senility. We become weak when we grow old. I remember when my 83-year-old grandmother was so weak that she walked around slowly and used a cane. Weakness in the church is an indication that we live in the old age of the church. We have a hard time getting around, and when we do, it takes us a lot of time while leaning on some artificial strength.

Inactivity is another mark. We do as little as we can and make up for it by talk.

## Focused on the Past

The worst of all signs is retrospection. The first four we probably cannot help, but the last one we can. Many churches are hindered by the presence of people who saw a better day once, and they cannot get over it. They look back and say, "But you should have heard so-and-so." No preacher has been able to do them any good since.

Retrospection means that you are always looking back. If the Lord had wanted you to look back, He would have put eyes in the back of your head. The church of Christ is now in that retrospective stage. We gaze back at what we call the golden age, where giants walked in the earth, and we seem like midgets compared with some of those Bible heroes. There is such a contrast between them and us that we are led to question whether we're really Christians at all. They saw God, and we seem to see only the reflection or the picture of God. They drank of the pure water that flowed from the hills of heaven, and we drink stale bottled water. They heard music, and we hear only the echo of it. However, we cannot go back.

Let nobody say, "I wish we could go back to . . ." If you do that, you shackle yourself and put a 100-pound ball and chain on your leg. I have never been guilty of thinking that I wanted to go back. I would not go back five minutes if I can help it. I do not believe that it would do me any good to go back. When I read the sweet story of old when Jesus was here among men, I think I should have liked to be with Him then. But then again, I would not go back there for all the world. I would rather live now than to live in the hour when Jesus put His hands on the heads of babies.

Even if I could, I would not want to go back to the days of John Wesley or Charles Finney or D. L. Moody. This is our day, if we know what to do with it. We have to be taught by the unbelieving philosophers like the great Ralph Waldo Emerson, who said, "This, like all times, is a very good one, if we but know what to do with it." He seemed to know what we Christians do not seem to recognize. We sniffle over a yesterday, and often those yesterdays were not as great as they might have been. We just hear about the best times. You read a book and you read the best things that happened in those days. Rarely do you read anything about the worst things that happened.

## The Church at Her Jordan

We stand today in a new age and you cannot recall any glories that might have been by any artificial means. You cannot by calling your church a Bible name bring back the Bible glory. It was an interior glow, and God never looked at clothes anyhow. You can have the interior power; anything God ever did for anybody, God will do for anybody else. Any blessing that God gave to Elijah or Abraham, God will give to us right now.

We stand at our Jordan, as Elisha stood at his. Our Jordan is a different Jordan, and each generation has its own Jordan. The Jordan that is there is turbulent and swift, determined and muddy, and it does not want to part; but Elisha parted it.

We have our own Jordan to cross. I think we ought to be moving forward, and there ought to be revival bursting out here and there. I think there ought to be more people at prayer meeting; I think there ought to be less worldliness in the church; I think there ought to be more devotion and worship—more of God and more fire.

There shines the glory for the church today. There is a Jordan rolling between us, and we need to say, "Where is the Lord God of Elijah?"

Elisha was there at the Jordan, and in his thinking, if he could only get Elijah, he could roll back the river and go across. What Elisha did not know was that Elijah's God was there, and he did not need Elijah. Likewise, Elijah is of no use to us today.

## God Does the Miracles

The question we need to ask is not, where is the Lord God of Elijah? The question we really need to ask is, who is the Lord God of Elijah?

If you do not know who God is and what God is like, your faith will never mount up.

This God of Elijah is a God who manifests Himself. Notice here that God manifested Himself to Elijah and to the people under Elijah's direction. The Lord God was tapping on the window all the time, trying to get through and trying to manifest Himself. He manifested Himself in fire, but He also manifested himself in the still, small voice of our conscience. He manifested Himself in providence and in prayer. God is ready to manifest Himself to us right where we are.

Religion searches around for God as if He were lost. In all their searching they never really find God. There are so many theological rabbit trails that never lead to the manifest presence of God.

"Manifest" means to show Himself. He is ready to take the veil away from Himself and shine through upon His church. The God of Elijah is the God who manifests Himself.

He is the God who works the miracles. Personally, I am not a miracle-monger, and I do not believe we ever ought to announce, "We're going to have a miracle tonight." God works miracles, but we cannot tell God what to do. God will work miracles when He needs to.

A miracle is an event divinely caused, an event in nature that does not have natural causes. An event, while not contrary to nature, rises above nature because the source is in God.

If Christianity is ever to survive, God had better work miracles. Every advancement of God in every country since the early church has been a miracle. Reading those stories one cannot help but see God opening doors that could never be opened by any natural means.

The whole life of Elijah was a miracle, from the ravens feeding him at the brook until it dried up to the widow woman feeding him and taking care of him, all the way up to his encounter with false prophets. Almost every step of the way was a miracle.

God was with Elijah.

God the Father Almighty manifests Himself to His people either inwardly or by miracles and whirlwinds. Either one way or another is necessary, which is why God does it.

## The Man to Whom God Shows Himself

This is who the Lord God of Elijah is. The next question is, where is the Lord God of Elijah?

Let me say that He is very near. He is here now waiting for us to fulfill certain conditions. Just as Elijah met those conditions and God manifested Himself to him, so too God is waiting on us.

Let me say that God is here as He was then and He was there then and that there is nothing to prevent us from seeing God do anything now that He did then. The Lord God of Elijah is here waiting for somebody as fearless as Elijah was.

### Fearless

Elijah was a fearless man of great courage. There is danger today that requires a lot of courage to have that Mount Carmel experience. It takes a lot of courage to stand out. Whenever we try to get along with each other, we never have any trouble and we never get into trouble. It always weakens us.

When Elijah was standing against the false prophets, we find hundreds of prophets of God hiding in a cave. Only one man stood up against the false religion, and that was Elijah. If all of those prophets hiding in the caves had the spirit of Elijah, they would have shaken Israel to its foundation. They would have frightened Jezebel back to Sidon where she belonged, and Ahab would have crawled in a hole somewhere and pulled it in after him. The power of God would have leaped out on Israel; but they were hiding. It takes courage to stand against the enemy.

God always used men of courage down through the years. It requires a great deal of courage to stand for God in an hour like this—to be a son of God among the sons of men; to be a citizen of heaven among the citizens of the world; to be a good man in a bad world and have faith in a world of unbelief; to be good in a world that loves to be bad. It takes courage, and

God is waiting for us to rise up with something of the fearlessness of Elijah.

## Dedicated

God is also looking for someone with the consecration of Elijah. That seems to be trite and commonplace today. Our dedication ought to be to God; and if God will find people completely dedicated to Him, He will begin working wonders this generation needs to see.

## Obedient

Then there was the obedience of Elijah. He went and did according to the Word of the Lord; and every time God spoke to him, he went and did according to the Word of the Lord. Because of this, God did according to the word of Elijah, and the two worked together in harmony. God said, "Elijah, do this," and he ran and did it. Elijah said, "Oh God, do this," and God moved and did it. God and Elijah worked together because Elijah listened to the Word of the Lord, and the Lord listened to the word of Elijah.

God is looking for obedient people. I mean positively obedient, not passively obedient, but intentional obedience.

A person can sit disobedient and lazy and sing every Sunday morning, "Have Thine own way, Lord, have Thine own way." That is passivity personified. God cannot have His own way unless you get up and do what He tells you to do. God having His way in your life means that when God says, "Do this," you do it. The church of Jesus Christ is cursed with passive obedience, which of course is disobedience.

While we are looking about for the rose-bordered way, Elijah took the tough way of faith and obedience and thus put himself on the spot. The way involves a kind of faith that Elijah had, a hazardous faith.

## Prayerful

Also, God is looking for someone as prayerful as Elijah. Elijah lived for prayer, he commanded in prayer and he claimed through prayer.

We do not want the good old days; we want the God of the good old days.

We all have electricity in our homes—a quiet power that will run all of our appliances. You cannot see it and you cannot hear it, but it is there, and you know it is there because when you are plugged into it, there is power.

God Almighty is with us. I do not hear Him, as I do not hear electricity. Nobody has ever seen Him, but He is here. How do we know He is here? Because if I meet the conditions that God has set, I get the power. There are conditions that need to be met. The Lord God of Elijah is our God today; He is the God and Father of Jesus Christ. He is a God who works miracles today, but there must be conditions met: the conditions are faith and obedience. Plug them into the mighty source and you will have the power that Elijah had.

The Lord God of Elijah is waiting for a fearless people, a consecrated people, an obedient people, a faith-filled and prayerful people. When He finds them, He begins to do for them what He did for others in days gone by.

*O God of Elijah, we long for Thee to do among us what Thou didst among those mighty prophets of old. May we so surrender ourselves today that Thou canst do in us and through us what only Thou canst do. In the name of Jesus, I pray. Amen.*

# 10

# THE SOVEREIGN CALL OF GOD

*And it came to pass, when they were gone over,*
*that Elijah said unto Elisha, Ask what I shall do for thee,*
*before I be taken away from thee. And Elisha said, I pray thee,*
*let a double portion of thy spirit be upon me.*

2 KINGS 2:9

Men become prophets not at their own whim but by the sovereign calling of God. If God does not call the man, he cannot carry God's message.

At our Bible college we had a dean of students who firmly believed this. When someone graduated from college, he rarely helped them find a place of ministry. One day someone confronted him with this and asked why he was not more helpful.

"If," the dean explained, "God has called that man to the ministry, God will open up the doors of ministry. If, on the other hand, mama called her son to the ministry, let mama find him a place of ministry."

Perhaps the man was a little rigid in this area, but he carried a right point. If God has called someone to ministry, nothing can keep that person from that ministry. Our problem today is that ministry has simply become a vocational choice. This has brought untold misery to the church. Ministry is not a vocational choice; it is a sovereign call of God upon a man's life. Nobody has any right to make a judgment in this area.

It is always wrong for us to judge values by size, but we constantly attempt to do that. In the Western world, we have the biggest things and the richest and the largest and the longest and the widest. We have sizes, all right, but still it is wrong to judge values by size.

A man can back up five tons of coal to your house, if you still use coal, and spend the day putting it in the coal bin. Yet, your wife wears on her finger something far more valuable than all the coal it took two men all day to put into your coal bin. Size and weight do not mean value.

Take the nation of Israel. Israel's importance did not lie in what she was as a people. It lay in what God had made her through His covenants. God takes that which is nothing and makes it something. People who always know where they are going are not following the Lord, because He cannot be predicted quite so perfectly as that. Israel thought they were something; but apart from God, they were nothing.

For years, Elijah had been the prophet to Israel. Although he was not much in himself, he held the most important position in his relationship to God and Israel.

Elijah is about to finish his work. When God calls a prophet home, or to any kind of work, He calls him in His way. It is our business to say goodbye to the past and face the future, knowing that we have been promoted.

## God Identifies the Replacement

God never takes away an Elijah without raising up an Elisha to fill his shoes. The work of God will never stop; you can be sure of that. God's servants go to their eternal reward, but the work of God continues. God was going to continue to bless Israel, even when Elijah was gone. The Lord would raise up another man, by the name of Elisha, to carry on that work.

Let me point out that some of God's present leaders are in the process of going. Some are within the last few years, and the temptation is to say, "If the Lord takes away His giants, what are we going to do?" God never takes away any Elijah without raising up an Elisha to fill his shoes. He never takes away a Moses without then raising up a Joshua. He never takes away a St. Paul without raising up a St. Augustine, or someone else, to take his place.

When Elijah was about to go, God was laying his hand on somebody else. God is putting His hand on somebody right now who is going to occupy the place of someone you look up to and think is so great—that mighty preacher, that mighty man of God. One of these days, God is going to take the breath out of his nostrils and he will be a lump of clay. That is all he ever was in the first place. All that he is, the good God gave him. When we look at all these mighty men God is going to take home, we know He is looking around for others to take their places. The people who are taking their places may not look that important to us by comparison.

# God Makes Nothing into Something

So, who is the Lord looking for? Some mighty giant who could walk out there like Hercules? No. When God bestows honor, He seldom turns to the mighty. Very rarely does God turn to the mighty when He wants to bestow honor.

The apostle Paul pointed this out when he wrote, "But God hath chosen the foolish things of the world to confound the wise; and God hath chosen the weak things of the world to confound the things which are mighty; and base things of the world, and things which are despised, hath God chosen, yea, and things which are not, to bring to nought things that are: that no flesh should glory in his presence" (1 Cor. 1:27-29).

God does not choose the obvious, but the one through whom He will get the most glory. The Scriptures, as well as church history, are full of this sort of thing.

Gideon was hiding away, threshing a little bit of grain in a cave, afraid of the Midianites, when God came to him and said, "Thou mighty man of valor" (Judg. 6:12). Surely, God must have smiled when He said those words to a man hiding away from the Midianites. Gideon did not believe it, of course. He would know a mighty man of valor when he saw one; and yet when God calls you, you are that. It is part of faith not to argue with God when He calls you out like He did Gideon.

Then there was David, the least likely of all his brothers. The prophet Samuel tried to anoint every other brother, but the Holy Spirit said, "That's not my man."

Finally, when they all stood around shrugging their shoulders and saying there has been a mistake somewhere, somebody remembered the youngest son, David. No possibility that it could be David; but when he came in, Samuel recognized right away that this was God's choice (see 1 Sam. 16).

God takes that which is nothing and makes something out of it.

Look at Peter the fishermen. Who would have picked Peter to be one of the apostles of Jesus? If there had been a vote somewhere, he would have been voted the least likely to be an apostle. God looked at him and said, "Peter, I have a job for you to do." He picked Peter and made him the great man that Scripture tells us about today.

When God takes a great man, He humbles him; and when He picks an unimportant man, He raises him. That is the way God does things.

The message always is more important than the messenger. The messenger must be worthy of the message, but the message continues after the messenger has gone.

## The Honor of God's Call

An important consideration in this regard is that the call of God always bestows honor. God never calls anyone down. He may call them down from their dizzy heights, as He called Zacchaeus to come down from the sycamore tree, because he should have never been up there in the first place. He may call them down, but He never calls a man to come beneath himself. He never calls anyone to move away from heights. He always calls us up higher.

When you move toward God, you are moving up; when you move away from God, you are moving down. God always calls us upward.

When God calls you to some kind of humble service—it may be working in a rescue mission—He has promoted you.

God called this man Elisha.

When we meet Elisha, he is out plowing. It was not particularly a high-status job, but it must have been quite a farm, for he had 12 yoke of oxen. From a human standpoint, there was nothing to recommend that Elisha follow in the footsteps of Elijah, that great prophet.

But, as Elijah passed by, God said to him, "There's your man." Elijah walked over to the field, took his mantle—the symbol of his office—and flung it toward Elisha. Destiny was passing along the road, and Elijah was in a position to hear from God.

Today, we are too flippant. We take things too lightly; we turn from one thing to another too easily. We do not think enough; we do not meditate enough; we do not dream enough; and we do not give God a chance to speak to us. The result is that when God may want to speak, He speaks quietly by nothing more than the wind from a mantle of the Holy Ghost flung in our direction. We cannot hear and notice because of the drama and the color and the noise and the speed at which we live.

Elisha was a man plowing in the field when destiny passed by in the person of an old prophet about to go home. Elijah waved his mantle quietly, but the response had to come from Elisha; it could not come from Elijah. It had to come from the man Elisha. When Elijah laid his hand on him, Elisha recognized that this was the man of God.

Elijah, that salty old prophet, was not going to be sentimental about it. He told Elisha to go back, saying, "What have I done to thee?"

Elisha recognized the call of God, turned his back on his old life and followed Elijah from that point on. I firmly believe that if you are where you are now because of your ingenuity and maneuvering, you are probably not where God wants you to be. The call of God is a divine moment that is impossible to replicate.

Elijah, himself, never knew where he was going to be. His life was a constant reaction to the voice of God. Elijah always went where God wanted him go.

## God's Call Brings Surrender and Obedience

Another consideration is that God is not going to do anything that runs contrary to His laws. God is consistent in everything, and there is a divine harmony about all He does.

God is not the author of confusion (see 1 Cor. 14:33); the Bible clearly insinuates that the devil is the author of confusion. God will not use a man who is not in conformity to the will of God. God will not use a person just because he is a big shot in the eyes of the world. God cannot use big shots. God can only use that man or woman who will finally surrender to the will of God and say as Isaiah said, "Here am I, send me" (Isa. 6:8).

When God calls a man, the man knows it. When God calls a man, he cannot die until he has done the work God has called him to do. If God calls a man to a work, and the man says yes, that man cannot die until that work is done. The man God calls is immortal until his work is done.

A man may never know when his work is done. Maybe the Lord will have a man start a work and then take him to heaven, and somebody else will carry it on in a way that he could not.

(Never judge God if some missionary dies young, or a worker in the church dies young.)

Elisha left everything—his job, his friends, his wages, his big farm—and he left it for good. He did not attempt to do the impossible. He did not seek to walk on both sides of the fence at the same time; he turned his back completely on his past.

Jesus told a parable about putting new wine in old bottles—old wineskins. He was emphasizing the futility of patching an old garment with new material. When you become a Christian, you cannot patch your Christianity onto your old life. You are to start over, turn your back on the past and follow the leading of the Lord.

Elisha said goodbye and turned his back on his former life. He put his life on the altar of obedience and surrender. He burned the bridge so he could never go back again. When God has called you, you kill the oxen, say goodbye to the old life, abandon the old business and go forward with God.

As long as you can hear those old oxen bellowing, there is a temptation to go back to the old life.

When God called the prophet home, He called him in His way. Likewise, when we are called, it is our business to say goodbye to the past and face the future, knowing we have been promoted. Accept God's call as a promotion. Burn the old bridges and fix it so you cannot go back; then serve God with all your heart.

> *My heart, O God, yearns for Thee and listens for that call that only comes from Thee. May I respond in such a way that I honor Thee before a world that is watching. Gratefully, in Jesus' name, amen.*

# 11

# THE DYNAMICS OF EXPERIENCING GOD

*Now it came to pass in the thirtieth year, in the fourth month,*
*in the fifth day of the month, as I was among the captives by the river*
*of Chebar, that the heavens were opened, and I saw visions of God.*

EZEKIEL 1:1

Today we have cheap religion passing for Christianity. This cheap religion consists of bits of poetry, a few flowers, a kindly smile and a deed done for your brother. That seems to be the Christianity flavor of the day.

The Christianity we have today that passes for the Christianity and the Bible, "Faith of our fathers living still in spite of dungeon, fire, and sword!" I do not know if it is possible to use language strong enough for its condemnation because it is not of the truth.

With the story of Ezekiel, we see the truth of the way God meets men.

Ezekiel was sitting by the river Chebar in utter dejection; all hope was gone. The light had gone out of his heart. When

Ezekiel was at the lowest point of his life, and there was nothing more he could do, he encountered God.

We do not know how long Ezekiel's encounter with God took; it could have been a brief moment, but it changed his life forever. As a result of that encounter and experience with God, Ezekiel became a voice of God to his generation.

Where are those voices today? Where are those men and women who have come to the end of self so that they can experience God in the Majesty of His revelation?

Today, we do not want that. We do not want the plow; we want the harvest. We do not want the night; we want the morning. We do not want the cross; we want the crown. Thomas à Kempis said, "The Lord has many lovers of His crown, but few lovers of His cross."

In the kingdom of God we want to reap the harvest and get every kind of benefit in order to get something for nothing. It just is not possible.

Along with this is a misconception of grace. Grace does not mean that salvation is not a costly thing. It simply means that out of God's goodness He gives grace to us who are unworthy of it. German pastor and anti-Nazi dissident Dietrich Bonhoeffer emphasized this in his modern classic *The Cost of Discipleship*. In it, he makes a distinction between cheap grace and costly grace. He wrote, "It is costly grace because it costs us everything, but it is free grace because it is freely given by God to people that do not deserve it."

Our fathers knew the distinction, but their poor, degenerate sons do not seem to recognize it.

Ezekiel, this man of God, was despondent and down; he was in that place of dejection and being stripped down.

Everything was taken from him, and he had nowhere to go and nowhere to lean. We are a tricky crowd, and if we can find anything human to lean on, we will lean on it. If we can find anybody to help us short of God, we will hunt everywhere else, and God is usually the last one asked.

God stands under the everlasting shadow of usually being the last one consulted. Sometimes people will get up and testify, "I have done everything, and all I can do now is trust God." The One we should go to first is usually the one we go to last. We are a tricky crowd, and that is why God sometimes has to take everything away from us to make us understand that He ought to be first.

David said, "The plowers plowed upon my back: they made long their furrows" (Ps. 129:3). That was an old countrified expression meaning that it hurts to have furrows plowed up your back; it hurts to have someone walking around on you with hobnailed boots. Ezekiel knew what that was all about. When he could not feel any worse, it was then that the heavens were opened and he saw visions of God.

## Whom God Has Stripped Let No Man Clothe

My advice is that if you are despondent about your spiritual life, or even if you are just a bit down, do not let the joy boys come and cheer you up. Do not let the chin chuckers come around and chuck you under the chin and say, "All is well, all is well." They have done the kingdom of God more harm by trying to make people clothed that God has stripped.

God strips a person, waiting for him to look up and receive the light; and then some joy-bell boy comes around wanting to

put a garment on him again. Leave the person in his naked-
ness before the great God Almighty; and when He clothes
the person, he will be clothed with golden garments.

Everybody wants the easy way out. The bookstores are
flooded with books written on how easy it is to be a Christian.
We preach sermons about how easy it is to be a Christian.
All lies. It is never a snap to carry a cross, and it is never easy
to follow the One who was opposed and rejected of men; but
there is joy in it. Paul spoke of it as "joy unspeakable and full
of glory" (1 Pet. 1:8). There are tears aplenty, but there is sun
that shines on the tears and makes the rainbow. A tearless
Christianity is no Christianity at all.

The heavens are closed for a variety of reasons, but there
is one ominous consequence, and that is that men are left to
themselves. God meant us to have Him, but the heavens are
closed, and now we are alone, without Him. The world is by
itself, and yet men without God nurse a groundless hope, a
hope that somehow things will come out all right, but they
will not. Anything that is worth having you will get from God.

Modern medicine and technology can help make people
live longer but cannot make them live happier. Regardless
of all the advancements in our society, the world is pretty
much a lonely crowd. It is not the presence of others that
cures loneliness; it is the presence of God.

Toward the end of his life, Charles H. Spurgeon com-
mented, "I can testify that never for 15 minutes since my
conversion have I been without a sense of the presence of
God." When you have God with you, you are conscious of
God being with you no matter where you are. You are conscious of it all the time, no matter what you may be doing.

These men of God met God in such a way that they never lost the sense of His conscious presence in their life. Their world was filled with God. It was for them a rising of the sun.

What happened when these men who were greatly used of God experienced God? They all had a sense of God, a consciousness of God in their midst, which can only be cultivated in the stillness.

## Be Still and Know that He Is God

We live in a society that has seeped into the church. It is full of all kinds of activity and noise. From the time you get up in the morning until you go to bed at night, there is activity and noise and chatter. In all of that, we cannot come to the place of getting to know God.

As long as we are satisfied with the status quo, we will never come to the point where we truly experience God as He desires to be experienced. The experience is always on God's terms, not ours.

It is not popular, but it is powerful. That is, we need to get still in order to experience God. David the psalmist understood this when he wrote, "Be still, and know that I *am* God: I will be exalted among the heathen, I will be exalted in the earth" (Ps. 46:10). It is in that stillness that we truly experience His presence.

Elijah discovered this. "And after the earthquake a fire; but the LORD was not in the fire: and after the fire a still small voice" (1 Kings 19:12). All the noise kept Elijah from hearing that "still small voice" speaking to him. How many of us are missing that voice because of all of the commotion in our life?

If we are willing to surrender that commotion and offer it on the altar, we might have a chance of hearing that "still small voice" speaking to us today.

Those men who were mightily used of God, who became a voice of God in their generation, heard that voice in the stillness and quiet of their own hearts.

## Have You Met with God Yet?

In looking at these great men of God, I notice that the details of their encounters with God were always sharp and clear to the individual. There was no mistake about it; God was speaking to them in a clarity that inspired obedience in their hearts. What we do not hear clearly, we are not willing to obey.

You must meet God. It is not simply that you can meet God; it is not simply that you might meet Him. You *must* meet God. This is the imperative if you are to be a voice to your generation. You do not have to travel the world looking for God or tap on a tree or rock to see if God is there, or climb up into heaven to pull God down into the depths. "But the word is very nigh unto thee, in thy mouth, and in thy heart, that thou mayest do it" (Deut. 30:14).

To tell people that they ought to meet God is never enough. They also need to be told how to meet God. It is through the gospel that we discover this. The gospel tells us that there is a door, and only one. Jesus Christ is that door, and through that door, we meet God. Christ takes God in one hand and man in the other and brings them together, introducing them, and man is restored in the favor and grace of God.

The Lamb of God taketh away the sins of the world. He died for the unjust that He might bring us to God. The gospel also tells us that we are saved by faith, through grace, and that not of works, lest any man should boast. It is at the cross of Jesus, at the open tomb of Jesus, and at the throne of Jesus that people really meet God.

The prophets of old clearly had met God. The presence of God appeared in their human intellect and illuminated to them the reality that is in God. This is what the Holy Spirit desires to do for us today. If we are to be the voice of God in our generation, we must be illuminated by the Holy Spirit, which invades the human intellect. We must walk by faith, not by sight.

Although this is a brief experience, it affects your life for as long as you live. You are never the same after you have encountered the presence of God.

I think one of the keys to this is first to repudiate all self-help. These are the days of the books that show how you can help yourself. It is not self that we want to help; rather, self is to be repudiated and put on the cross.

In the world of medicine, self-medication is never a good idea. No medical doctor loves to hear that you have been self-medicating. It is never a good idea when you try to fix yourself, and it goes double in the area of the spiritual. You cannot make yourself holy. All self needs to be repudiated.

We also need to lift up our eyes; when we do so, we will see a smiling Father looking down. The Christian life that you can have is so much more wonderful than the Christian life you now have.

The greatest crime in our generation is the fact that we have too many people who think they know how to fix every situation. We have counselors and psychologists who are trying to keep man together. Thank God that Ezekiel had nobody who could help put him back together. All he had was God. All he needed was God.

If we are going to be a voice in our generation, God will guide us down the path where all we have is God. Ezekiel was such a man, and when the heavens opened for him, he experienced God in ways that are beyond human calculation. As soon as you can figure God out, you have not met the true God and Father of our Lord Jesus Christ.

*Dear God, may we surrender and hand everything over unto Thee. May we refuse to help ourselves in order that You can lift us up into the heavens that we might experience Your presence as we could never experience it before. This I pray in Jesus' name, amen.*

# 12

# WE NEED PROPHETS,
# NOT PROMOTERS

*And God said unto Moses, I AM THAT I AM: and he said, Thus shalt thou say unto the children of Israel, I AM hath sent me unto you.*

EXODUS 3:14

What prepared Moses for his great work was what I refer to as the crisis of encounter. Out of this crisis came a sense of the sacred. Perhaps the reason there is such a lack of reverence today is because most people have never met God in this way.

For the most part, the average Christian does not know that there is such a thing as meeting God in the crisis of encounter as Moses did. We are brought into the kingdom of God by smooth-talking people with marked New Testaments that tell us logically how to get converted. Everything is casual, and nothing disrupts our normal way of living.

In my mind, there is nothing more awe-inspiring than Moses standing before the burning bush. No matter how many times I have read this passage of Scripture, I always come away with a sense of wonder and astonishment. This man Moses became what we know him to be because of his encounter at the burning bush.

Moses was one of the great leaders of all time. He served as a prophet, a lawgiver and a great leader of his people. He received from God the greatest moral code ever given to mankind—the Ten Commandments. Someone once said that the Constitution of the United States was the greatest document struck off by the mind of man. A great system of law lies there, but the greatest of all that was ever given by God came through Moses.

"This is that Moses, which said unto the children of Israel, A prophet shall the Lord your God raise up unto you of your brethren, like unto me; him shall ye hear" (Acts 7:37).

This man Moses was also an emancipator of the Jewish people, a leader, a statesman and a teacher of the ages. All this he became, and for this he was already fairly well developed. This man was so great, it was said of him that he had been educated in all the wisdom of the Egyptians. He received everything that Egypt could possibly give to a man.

Then Moses had a postgraduate course, which I believe is more to be desired than his education at the feet of the great teachers of Egypt. He went to the school of silence—to the sheep and to the stars and to the heavens above. All through the evening, before sleep overtook him, he listened to the silence.

When you want pure loneliness, absolute solitude, look at the stars. The stars make no noise; they simply burn on in their magnificence. Moses had occasion to look at the stars all during the evening and all night long, if he cared to, and whenever he woke up in the night.

God took this man Moses out of the noise and put him in the silence where he could hear his own heartbeat. Moses learned some lessons there that he could not have learned anywhere else. He learned to know himself.

We moderns know everything but ourselves. We do not know ourselves because we cannot get quiet enough. The reason we pay so little attention to the City of God that shines yonder, the starry universe, is that there is so much noise and distraction.

Even in this place, there was something Moses had to learn that he could never have learned at the court of Pharaoh or from looking at the stars or from listening to the sheep. Only one thing prepared Moses for his great work, which he could not have done without preparation. That one thing was God giving Moses an encounter with Himself.

God wanted Moses to meet Him face-to-face and learn a sense of sacredness.

## The Sacred in Today's Church

The greatest loss modern man has suffered is not the loss of limb or of home, as tragic and terrible as those things might be. The loss of loyalty and the loss of law keeping are losses that spring out of another loss—the loss of the sense of sacredness.

I grieve when I come into the average gospel church, because there is an absence of God in that fellowship. There is so little of the sense of God in the average church today. You never bow your head with reverence unless you deliberately discipline yourself to do it, because there is no sense of sacredness.

Anything goes, and this is the loss that is too terrible ever to be appraised. The world has hidden God from our sight, and secularism has taken over. We have secularized God, the gospel, worship and Christ. I insist that this is a great and tragic loss, and no great man can come forth out of that. No great movement can spring out of that kind of a thing. God may have to sweep it away and start somewhere else.

The only thing that is going to help us today is that which Moses experienced. It enabled him to be the prophet of God that God needed at that time. The cure for our problem today is to meet God in the crisis of encounter.

## We Need a God Encounter

How did God reveal Himself to Moses? God revealed Himself as fire. God is inscrutable. He is ineffable and cannot tell us what He is, only what He is like. Therefore, God tells us that He is like fire.

God is in fire, though the Scripture says our God is a consuming fire. It does not mean that God is fire physically or ontologically. Although the theologians would say that God is fire, we know that God is not fire. Fire can bring down a building or cook your stew. God is not that kind of a fire. But fire is the nearest thing to being like God that God can think of to tell His children what He is like.

Therefore, God appeared here, in the twilight, in fire, and Moses knelt as God spoke out of the midst of the bush. Moses saw, felt and experienced God in that encounter, and God commissioned Moses to deliver Israel, to receive the law and to organize the greatest nation in the world, out of which the Messiah would come. He was able to do all this because he met God in the fire.

The effect of this experience greatly changed Moses. The fire in the bush was God dwelling within the fire and shining out through the fire. It was the presence of God, and Moses experienced God there. God was no longer merely an idea to Moses.

## Distinguish Knowledge Versus Experience

To the average person today, God is just an idea, nothing more. Up to this time in Moses' life, God was just a thought. Moses perceived God in an intellectual way. Now, he experienced God personally.

There are two types of knowledge. First there is the knowledge that comes from the Scripture, and then there is the knowledge that comes from experience. You can describe a thing and have knowledge of it, and you can give knowledge to others by describing it. But it is another thing to go through what you describe. It is one thing to describe the battle, but the man going through the battle actually experiences it. And the strange thing is that the one who has actually experienced it says very little about it.

Moses experienced the living God. God was not history to Moses; God was a living personality.

The tragic breakdown in fundamental circles is that we have substituted doctrine for experience. The Bible was never given to be an end in itself. The Bible was given to be a path leading us to God; and when the Bible has led us to God, and we have experienced God in the crisis of encounter, the

Bible has done its work. It is not enough that you should memorize Scripture. Some Christians memorize the Word of God but never meet the God who wrote the Word. They can quote whole chapters but have never been inspired by the same Holy Spirit that inspired the Word.

The Bible can only be properly understood through the Spirit that inspired it. For me to memorize whole passages of Scripture is useless unless I, by means of those Scriptures, meet God in the crisis of encounter.

## During and After the Burning Bush

We can know God as Moses knew the burning bush; we can know God for Himself.

Let me point out some lessons Moses received from this fire in the bush.

### Helpless in the Presence of the Fire

First, the fire dwelling in the bush was a type of the Lordship of Jesus. Paul calls this the rich mystery and hope of glory, which is Christ in you (see Col. 1:27). The fire dwelt in the bush. It was in an acacia bush, and the bush was perfectly helpless in the fire.

You will never know God as you should know Him unless you are helpless in His hands, unless you cannot escape Him. As long as you can run, you are not in God's hands. As long as you can back out, as long as there is a bridge behind you so that you can retreat, you are not in God's hands.

We often make God the last resort; but here was a bush that could not back out of it, could not get out of there.

It was caught there; and the happy Christian that has been caught by the Lord and cannot escape does not want to escape. He has burnt all of his bridges from every direction, and there is no other way to go.

You can walk with the Lord as long as things are normal, but when you experience a tight spot, it is nothing to fool with. Thank God that this bush was caught, and the fire was in the bush.

### Purified in the Presence of the Fire

Another thing that strikes me here is that the fire purified this bush. All the bugs and larva, and the wind—all perished in the fire. Turn a fire loose in that bush for five minutes and there is not a living thing in it that can survive. There would not have been a bush if God had not preserved it. That fire preserved the bush but slew all the external matter. No one can stand before the fire of God's presence. God is the holiness that we need.

Some people think holiness is something you get and that you take out with you and carefully guard it lest you lose it. Holiness is nothing else than the holy God dwelling in a human being's heart. The heart will be holy because God is there, and God is holy. The bush had no purity of its own; and if the fire went out of the bush, as it probably did after God had given His demonstration to Moses, the bugs soon came back.

The purity and holiness we desperately need are by the presence of God; they come from an encounter with God; they come by the fire of God in the human heart. Cleansing and purity come by the indwelling Christ.

Christ is not our sanctifier; He is our sanctification, which is another issue altogether. He is our holiness. So, if He dwells there, as a fire dwelt in the bush, we have a living encounter and experience. The man indwelt by Christ will be a pure man, because Christ in him is pure, living out through him.

### Transformed in the Presence of the Fire

The bush was just a scrub thorn bush, and I imagine there were millions of them there. Maybe there were hundreds of thousands of them scattered over the broad face of the wilderness, and they did not amount to anything. The flame, however, transfigured this particular bush until it became the most famous bush in all of history. However, its glory was not on its own but was derived from the indwelling fire. It took on a glow, a glory, and it has held that glory all down these years.

Men talk about the burning bush; artists paint the burning bush; we preach about the burning bush. Why? Because it was a great bush? No, because it was a great fire in the bush.

One of the byproducts of Christianity is that God takes people who have never amounted to anything and never will, and by living in them, transforms them, giving them meaning and significance.

A man may be just an average person, faceless and without significance, but let Jesus Christ get hold of that man, let the glory of the Lord get into that life, and the man takes on significance immediately.

### Protected in the Presence of the Fire

Another thing is that the fire protected this bush. No evil could come to that bush. Nobody can hurt a Christian—nothing and nobody can get through to a Christian—unless the Lord wants it to.

When the devil wanted to tempt Job, he complained to God and said, "God, You have a hedge around that man." He asked permission to get through, and God opened the hedge a little, and the devil slipped through and went to tempt Job.

No child of God can be touched if he has the fire dwelling in him.

What was it that protected the bush?

It was the fire in the bush. It did not need any wire fence or glass encasing, because nobody bothered the bush while the fire was in it. Nobody attacked the bush, because the bush was perfectly safe while the fire dwelled in it.

Thank God, our protection is by the indwelling fire.

**Made Beautiful in the Presence of the Fire**

Many years after this burning bush experience, Moses prayed a wonderful prayer: "And let the beauty of the LORD our God be upon us: and establish thou the work of our hands upon us; yea, the work of our hands establish thou it" (Ps. 90:17). When Moses saw that beautiful blaze in the twilight, he said, "I will turn aside now and see this great sight."

That attractiveness is the great and mighty need of religion today. More than any other thing, we need the sense of sacredness that brings beauty to light. One of the tragedies of the hour is unlovely orthodoxy.

# Those Who Are Called to Do God's Work

To anyone going out into religious work, you are called to be a burning bush, not to imitate a movie actor. You are not called to be great; you are called to be beautiful. The beauty may be in the fire or in your boldness or in your courage. Your call could be a burning bush, and I would seriously recommend to all who feel themselves called to do God's work to shun the coarse ways of the cheap gospel and the amateur. Stay away from them.

We are suffering today in evangelical circles from an epidemic of amateurism. Anybody who can talk can get up and talk. Coarseness, ignorance, cheap humor, a flash of wit at times to wake up an audience; I say, shun it and stay away from it.

We already have enough promoters; we need prophets. We already have enough organizers; we need men who have met God in the crisis of encounter.

Do you want to be that fire at any cost? The rank and file of the half-saved will think you are a fanatic.

I believe there are many crazy people in heaven, because everybody who truly meets God is branded as being a little bit wacky. The sanest man is a man who knows God the most; the sanest mind is the mind in which the fire dwells the most perfectly.

When you start to seek God in the crisis of encounter, people will say, "He's lost his mind." After you are established and get your feet down, and something goes wrong in their house, the phone will ring and they will say, "There's trouble over here. Could you come?"

The Lord is calling His people to the Spirit-filled life; He's calling them to a consecrated life, to a life committed to a point where they cannot back out and do not want to.

The question is, do you want to be one of them?

*O God of the fire, burn in my life today as You have never burned there before. Set my life aflame with the holiness of Thy presence. I pray this, O God, in Jesus' name. Amen.*

# 13

# The Privilege of Being Sent of God

*There was a man sent from God, whose name was John.*
*The same came for a witness, to bear witness of the Light,*
*that all men through him might believe.*

JOHN 1:6-7

The greatness of the man John did not lie in him but in his office and his privilege.

Abraham saw our Lord's day and was glad. But John the Baptist lived in that day, and that made him greater than Abraham.

David played his harp and sang of the Coming One who would be wounded and pierced but would rise again and sing among his brethren. But John the Baptist was there; he saw Him and felt Him.

Isaiah sang of One who would come born of a virgin and grow up as a root out of a dry ground. But John the Baptist touched the One Isaiah prophesied and baptized Him. His privilege was greater.

Malachi said He should suddenly come to His temple and sit as upon a fire. But John the Baptist actually walked in that Temple, and though that particular passage probably refers to the second coming of Christ, yet that same purifier of silver was there at His first coming, and John the Baptist was present and saw this. John saw Him and touched Him and heard Him and actually baptized Him and gave Him His start.

The privilege of John was greater than that of any of the rest.

It might have been said of John the Baptist that he was the greatest, but John did not say that. It might have been said that he was the strongest; I do not know whether he was. It might have been said that he was the wisest or the most gifted or the most eloquent, but Scripture did not say that. It said that John the Baptist was sent, and that was John's unspeakably high honor.

It was a higher honor for John than anything else to say that he was sent of God. The coming of this man sent of God was an inestimable blessing, and an unspeakable treasure to the world.

## Men Who Were Sent of God

God sends forth His men.

There was a man sent from God whose name was Noah. He was a just man who built himself an ark and saved himself and his family and saved the human race from extinction.

There was a man sent of God whose name was Abram. He came from Ur of the Chaldees, and was following nothing but the light in his own heart and the dim vision of the God of his father.

There was a man sent of God named Moses, who took that nation when it was lost in Egypt, in darkness and bondage, and led that nation across the Red Sea and into the wilderness. He guided and cherished and nursed and cared for that nation for 40 years.

When he died, there was a man sent of God whose name was Joshua, and Joshua gathered that nation as a hen gathers her chicks and took that nation across the river and established them in the land God had promised to Abraham, Isaac and Jacob.

There was a man sent of God whose name was David. He reached into his own heart and tore out the strings and set those strings in the windows of the synagogues for 1,000 years. The winds of persecution blew across them and made song for the Jewish worshipers. When the veil of the temple was rent, the Holy Ghost had those same heartstrings taken from the heart of David and strung them in the windows of the churches. Today you cannot sing without having David singing. There was a man sent of God whose name was David; he taught the world to sing, and the world has been singing David's songs ever since.

We could go on to mention Peter, Paul, Martin Luther, and men of God all the way down to our day. You can go down the line and take any list you happen to be fond of. Wherever men have done things for God, there was a man sent of God. They were men who could work with people, but they were men who always worked above people because they were sent of God.

No higher honor could ever come to any man than this, and here is where we develop our lessons and example from this man John.

## What Did God See in John?

To be owned of God and commissioned of God, to be empowered by God and sent of God is the highest honor that could be bestowed upon anyone.

Based on this, I want to know why God could use a man like John the Baptist the way He did. If God could use John the Baptist, He can use you and me today. What was it that God was looking for that He found in John the Baptist?

### A Man of Solitude

The basic thing God saw in John the Baptist was a man of solitude. He was in the desert until the time of his showing forth unto Israel.

I am not sure that John the Baptist would ever have fit into our time. He did not wear a suit; the language he spoke was not eloquent; he could not quote from the poets. But he had been in the desert with his God, in solitude, and he came out of his solitude to break the silence like a drumbeat to the trumpet sound. All gathered to hear this man who had been with God.

John the Baptist went into the silence and went to school with God, and with the stars, the howling winds and the sun. The trouble with us is that we cannot get quiet enough to wait on God. We have the idea that if we are not talking, something's wrong. Somebody has to be talking all the time. Someone has to be making a rattling noise of some sort.

God could use John the Baptist because He could get hold of him. He could stop him; He could slow him down long enough to get on board.

Most people never really find themselves. They are not meditating; they are not serious minded. The result is that they have to have company around them all the time. One philosopher said that the more you have inside of you the less you need people around you. If you do not have anything inside, you have to compensate for your inner vacuity by surrounding yourself with a bunch of noisemakers. Most people live like that. They cannot afford to live by themselves. They cannot get off anywhere and be still.

If you do not practice the art of holy solitude, you will not be worth anything in the kingdom of God. There must be silence, and John the Baptist was in the desert until the time for his showing forth unto Israel. Had he been adjusted to all the ways of the world, he never would have met God in the silence.

In the book of Job we read, "There was silence, and I heard a voice" (Job 4:16). I believe that the abrasive action of our culture has taken the character out of many a man, reducing him to a shiny dime among all the dimes of the world. He is shiny from much use and too much contact. He has lost it all because he has been too many places, seen too many people and made too many contacts.

If you get alone and let your knees make contact with the ground, and you stay there awhile, it will do more good than anything else.

The secret of John the Baptist was that he got on his knees and he looked upward and waited all day long on God in the desert while the wind and the dust blew about him.

## A Man of Simplicity

Another reason why God could honor John the Baptist was his simplicity. John had his raiment of camel's hair, and his food was locusts and wild honey.

There is something to be said for simplicity. I know that some go too far, like some Quakers, although I have admired them in many ways. If only we could be simple again.

John the Baptist had simplicity. He came dressed plainly and did not attempt to impress anybody. We live in a day when people, especially preachers, brag about themselves. As we begin to brag about ourselves, God disowns the whole mess and has nothing more to do with us. John the Baptist never bragged. He just walked around simply doing the will of God.

## A Man of Vision

Another reason has to do with vision. John the Baptist could see what God wanted him to see.

When he baptized the Lord Jesus, he saw the Holy Spirit descend like a dove and remain upon Jesus. Nobody else saw that, but John did. He had the vision to see what God was doing at that moment.

What is needed today is the opening of our eyes. The man with the open eyes can see what the man of no vision can never see.

Go out into the country with a hunter and he will see things the common man with dim vision can never see. The city man sees nothing at all except a few trees, bushes and leaves. The hunter sees beyond this to the prey at hand.

The woeful thing about having vision is that it always puts you out of gear with your time. John the Baptist was a man of vision in the midst of men who had no vision at all. John knew where he was in his time and was not going to be carried away by the drift of the hour.

Read a few magazines, listen to a few programs on radio or TV and you will know that religion has its direction. It has its vogue that begins when every little old preacher turns his head like a willow tree bough in that one direction, afraid to look the other way because it happens to be that the wind of religious vogue in that hour is roaring out of that direction, so everybody turns in that direction. The magazines take it up, the radio programs take it up, the preachers take it up, the laymen take it up, and money gets behind it because the wind is blowing from that direction.

Then, some partly bald-headed guy sees the mistake of it all and turns his face to the wind. Every man that has any vision is looking into the wind and does not give up to the trends of the time. He stands for God and New Testament Christianity in an hour when everybody is blowing in the other direction.

We need a few prophets who will dare to stand up and face the other way, who will see the drift in another direction altogether.

John the Baptist did not take his identity from the world around him, but from his focus on God above him. He was not caught up in the vogue of his times. Rather, he challenged the times with the ever potent, "Thus saith the Lord."

John was not quoting the latest best-selling book or the most popular person in religious circles. He was not aligning himself with the popular leaning of his day. His message came from God.

## A Man of Courage

Another reason why God could honor John the Baptist was because of his courage. He had to have courage when he stood up to the Jewish leaders and said, "You generation of vipers." That certainly was not a polite way of getting the congregation to like you.

Here was a man who was willing to confront the opposition, regardless of where it came from.

Many of us will not be sent of God because we do not have courage. We are afraid of being unique and different. Preachers are afraid of losing members from their congregation. They are afraid they will lose public esteem and be criticized. Christians are afraid of losing friends, afraid of losing reputation and income, afraid somebody will not like it.

God Almighty called His sheep; He did not call mice. The figurative sheep does not hold when it comes to prophets and soldiers and warriors in this day of declension and sin. God sometimes straps a buckler on his sheep, stands him up on his two hind legs, and turns him out, and by some miracle changes him from being a sheep into being a roaring lion. He sends him out to be a Luther or a Finney to a generation of vipers.

## A Man of Humility

We also have to look at the humility of John the Baptist. This was another reason why God could honor him as He did. He allowed Christ to displace him completely, and it is important that we understand this about John the Baptist. He allowed Jesus to displace him in everything.

John's testimony, recorded in John 1, shows us that he said words to the effect, "I am not the Christ. I am not Elijah. I am a voice sounding in the wilderness. I am just a voice sent crying in the wilderness, and I am not even talking about myself. I am talking about another One who is to come after me; and when He comes, He will be seen to be so great by comparison that I will be happy to get down, and I will not even feel worthy to loosen His shoes."

That was John the Baptist, and his ministry was over when Jesus came. John said, "Behold, the Lamb of God." He directed all eyes away from himself to Jesus and then faded out of the picture and said, "I must decrease while He must increase" (see John 3:30).

That minister who can do a great work and quietly fade out of the picture and let someone else take over is rare among men today. John the Baptist was that kind of a man. He did not want anything for himself.

The prophet that God honors is the one who has stopped bragging about himself and begins to talk about the Lamb of God who takes away the sin of the world. If that Lamb of God gets all the glory, they delight in it. They ask no glory for themselves, only to be present and hear the Bridegroom's voice.

That was John; and if you want God to send you, and you want the high honor of having it said that there was a man sent from God, then you must be humble, for God sends only the humble. The proud send themselves, but the humble are sent of God. I would not desire to be engaged in religious activity if I did not know I was sent of God. Unless I knew I was sent, I would not engage in any of the activities of religion today.

John the Baptist was sent of God because he loved solitude, simplicity, had vision, courage and humility. The God of John the Baptist is the God of this hour, and nothing has changed for the man sent of God. His qualifications have not been altered. God has not declared anything new from the day He made those qualities to mark His man. What marked a man back then will mark His man today.

*May we humbly bow before Thee, O God, as John of old did. Send us forth, O blessed Master, to a world that desperately needs Thee today. Amen.*

# 14

# THE VOICE OF A
# PROPHET IN THE
# WILDERNESS

*He said, I am the voice of one crying in the wilderness,
Make straight the way of the Lord, as said the prophet Esaias.*

JOHN 1:23

No prophet had been in Israel for 400 years. Malachi, the messenger, was the last one, and then Israel went into decline. Since then, no voice, no inspiration, only the faithful passing on of the doctrines of the Word taught by teachers telling what others said they had seen and heard. For 400 years, there had not appeared a man who had seen anything himself. He was forced to tell what others had seen and heard.

These were the custodians of theology, and they served an important place. They faithfully told what others had seen, declared what others had heard, but they themselves had neither seen nor heard.

Then came John the Baptist, who gave a very frank and illuminating testimony about himself: "I am not the Christ, but I have been sent before him" (see John 3:28). He had been preaching in the wilderness and was attracting a wide following and getting much attention.

These custodians of orthodoxy were disturbed by the appearance of a man who did not fit into their pattern. They sent to inquire whether he was one of the expected ones. Evidently, their prophetic expectations included three major figures: Christ, Elijah and "that prophet." This exhausted the list of the expected ones by these custodians of prophetic truth.

Here comes a man who is not Christ, and he is not Elijah, and he is not that prophet; and they who had fawned over the Scriptures said, "We are sorry, we have no reservations for you."

They could not figure out where John the Baptist fit into their understanding of the prophetic scheme of things.

John the Baptist did not fit into their plans, because they wanted to be let alone and did not want anybody to come and disturb them morally. What they wanted is what many people want today—for God to conform to their religious pattern. People are perfectly willing to go along with God as long as God will be good and conform to their pattern.

It took centuries to figure out their pattern. They had a long tradition behind them, and it would not be becoming of God to upset that pattern or destroy that tradition or do anything that was not on that agenda. They wanted God to approve and justify them. They did not want a prophet voice to come that would disturb them. They wanted to be let alone, but John called them to righteousness: "I am the voice of one crying in the wilderness, 'Prepare ye the way of the Lord'" (John 1:23).

The "wilderness" is the setting of John the Baptist's ministry.

The word "wilderness" here does not have the same meaning as it has when he said he was in the desert until his showing unto Israel. There the word "desert" or "wilderness" was identifiable, a piece of terrain that one could mark on a map and know where it was found. Here, as is often true in the Bible, after a literal use of the word follows a figurative use as an illustration.

John is now the voice of one crying in the wilderness, which refers to the moral condition of Israel.

In that context, a wilderness has certain characteristics.

## What Characterized Israel's Moral Wilderness

The first characteristic that comes to mind is that the wilderness is a thing of *chaos*. Go to a national park and you will find order; then go into a wilderness and you will find disorder.

Then there is *waste*, for these were deserts, and whole sections had no grass. Consequently, nothing lived in those sections. Without purpose or significance, they just existed.

A thread of *uncertainty* runs through it all. A wilderness, not like our Western deserts or even like the Sahara, but burnt over, beaten out, filled with green briars of all kinds, weeds and bitter grass here and a scrub bush there. Just a confused wilderness with no order whatsoever.

Another characteristic of the wilderness here is the *purposelessness* of it all. Some parts of the wilderness seemed as if God had dumped a truckload of stuff He did not need and just piled it up there. No purpose whatsoever in it, and it had no meaning.

There is also the wild *undomesticated* quality of the wilderness. Nobody obeys any arbitrary laws around there. Nobody comes when you whistle, lies down and turns over when you tell them to.

The wilderness is all wild. So we have confusion, disorder, waste and purposelessness, and John had all that in mind when he used the word "wilderness." He knew it and knew it well. That is what John saw in Israel. That is what God sent him to tell Israel.

I think I am seeing something like that today, and I hope enough people will see it before long who will do something about it. John saw what the religious leaders of Israel never dreamed could be true. He saw what the faithful custodians of orthodoxy never dreamed of. They saw themselves one way when God saw them another way. John saw them the way God saw them, and John and God were right. It was the voice of one crying in the wilderness.

It would not be worthwhile for us to vex our righteous souls concerning the conduct of the Pharisees and scribes and Levites, and all the rest who have been filling graves for many centuries. There is the present condition of the wilderness—a condition that parallels Israel when our Lord came, and that is my primary focus here.

## Technical Progress Does Not Improve Morality

Not too long ago, we were taught, tragically so, that the world was becoming better. We were told that the world is getting better because man is able to cure rabies, for instance. He is well on his way to cure diabetes and other diseases. Furthermore, man can do so many things he wasn't able to do before.

Because man has become a brilliant toymaker, we believe that the toys man makes are good. He can reach up and pull down the jagged lightning and put it in a box or run it along wires and send the voice along the wires. Then he can send that jagged lightning out without any wires from place to place.

Solomon was certainly right when he said, "Lo, this only have I found, that God hath made man upright; but they have sought out many inventions" (Eccles. 7:29).

Look at what this toymaker has been able to do throughout the years—everything from a rag doll to a radio to a telephone and then on to the automobile and airplane and way beyond. We are able to take a soybean and turn it into a suit of clothes from the skin out. We take glass that used to shatter when you hit it and bend it over and wear it. We are toymakers of the world. We make wonderful gadgets now. This is the generation of the gadget gurus.

## Modern Man's Greatest Failure

Through it all, we have overlooked one little thing. Along with man's strange and wonderful ability to take the forces of nature and combine them to make modern toys to make life easier, we have been led to believe that along with our progress in scientific subjects we should also have advanced in moral matters. That notion is our greatest failure.

Is it not strange that the generations that have had the most advancement in science and technology have also been the most morally despicable generations? A case in point is the degradation of womankind all over the civilized world. It has been overlooked, excused and laughed off.

Take the man with gangrene in his leg. If he could get enough people to glorify it and pay him to exhibit it, write books and poems about it and sing jive songs about it, we soon could glorify gangrene. The gangrene, however, will kill its victim just as sure as there is a God in heaven. Unless he cuts the gangrene out and gets rid of it all, it will kill him. You can never negotiate terms with gangrene.

To violate the laws of God is to bring pollution to the poor of the race. To continue this and excuse it and justify it, and not repent of it, and build it into our reasoning and write books around it is to glorify something that will kill us as sure as we live.

Think about how many crimes are being committed every minute of the day, and how many murderers are never caught.

When the moral philosophy of the world becomes such that he can do his evil and get on the front page, then God will withhold assent no longer, and we will rot from within so that when we say it is the wilderness we have the facts before us. We are surrounded by this wilderness.

If that were all, then I would say thank God for a pure church in the midst of all of this wickedness. I cannot say that and tell the truth. For the Christian church, instead of floating high above it all, free and clean and separated from it, her poor old boat has sprung a leak and the church and the world have become so mixed up that you can scarcely tell one from the other. The world has so affected our moral standards.

Christians say they believe in Christ but do not change their moral standard scarcely at all. These leaders like to preach to the Levites. You know the Levites defended themselves. They wanted to be let alone and approved. They did not want to be disturbed. They wanted to go to church because it was so peaceful there, and they could feel so good. All around them, however, the wilderness conditions were prevailing.

In our day, we preach the gospel and make converts, but we make converts to the wilderness.

If God should raise up a John the Baptist today, one of the first things he would set before us is to be deeply disturbed. Perhaps even angered.

Basic honesty compels me to say that I believe this, and if I am wrong, God will have to show me. Compared to what you ought to be, how much of this disorder is in your life? How much waste is there in your life? How much waste of the vital gifts of God? Waste of abilities and life and time? The wilderness is characterized by waste spaces that are no good to God or man.

Barrenness is part of the wilderness; nothing matures in the wilderness. Nothing much grows there except weeds. If there is any fruit it is scrubby, any grain is inferior grain.

I believe it would be better to have never been born than to be born once and only once. More than that, how tragic to be born twice and yet have no fruit to show for your Christian faith! How tragic to go our way never having really accomplished anything. Nobody in the earth will thank God that you lived.

You skinned through by the grace of God, but nobody will be sad when you go except your immediate circle of loved ones, and that is only emotional attachment.

Think of the wild plants growing today in the desert, and think of the wild plants that grow in many churches today. Plants of the flesh and of the world grow there. We are supposed to be a garden of God, but we are of formless wilderness in some instances, and those wild plants will only be cut down and thrown into the fire.

The drowsiness is upon us; we are not awake to see this. We are like a man who has been asleep only a short time and is desperately tired, and the cry of "fire, fire" partially awakens him but not enough for him to know what is going on. Many a man is in peril because he could not shake the drowsiness from his eyes in the moment of peril. Many of these never repented. Some did; a good many did so when our Lord Jesus was finally revealed. But the masses did not support the purpose of God and never repented.

I wonder how it will be today. I wonder whether we can shake off this drowsiness. What is it going to take to open our eyes to the church's moral condition? We are so busy with our jobs and raising our children and going to school and keeping up with programs and reading as much as we think we ought to and going to so many places without little social engagement. We have become so busy that we forget that there is a wilderness. The spirit of the wilderness is settled upon the churches of Christ as well as upon the great world around us.

There is a voice calling. God's voice speaks whatever He can, through whomever He can. God is trying to say to us a "voice crying in the wilderness." Now what are we going to do? Are we going to defend ourselves, or surrender? Are we going to obey and repent?

A drowsiness lies over churches today. Do you think this is a condemnation of churches? No, absolutely not. I believe in every little bit of good I see everywhere in the world, and I love it. I am the first one to come to its defense. I still think that if

God does not create some man who can be a voice to disturb within the next few years, that which we call fundamentalism will be liberalism, and modernism will be called atheist.

We are already on our way down. Decomposition asks no questions once it gets started. Cells break down, gases get released and the smell rises. It asks no questions, plays no favorites and has no partiality toward anyone. When putrefaction sets in it goes right on until the job is finished unless the Great Physician, who now is near, the sympathizing Jesus, is permitted to take His sharp knife and cut it out.

I would rather never preach again than to merely be an echo of an echo, a reflection of a life long gone. I want to find out what is wrong and then go after that. I want to identify the drowsiness upon the nation, the drowsiness upon the churches. This drowsiness is a characteristic of the wilderness around us.

Let us pray that God will make a reformation within His church that will purify His people—make them a separated people, a holy and Spirit-filled people, a biblical people, no matter what they call themselves. A people God can use.

*Dear God, may there be a mighty move upon my heart to separate me from the encroaching wilderness separating me from Thee. Speak so to my heart that I might be a voice to this generation. Amen.*

# 15

# THE AGENDA OF
# A PROPHET

*The next day John seeth Jesus coming unto him, and saith,*
*Behold the Lamb of God, which taketh away the sin of the world.*

JOHN 1:29

John the Baptist was called the forerunner simply because he ran before. When kings traveled in those days, they sent a man before them to announce their coming. John the Baptist was the herald of the coming King, the forerunner of King Jesus. He ran before to alert the populace and say that He was coming.

John, however, is not to be understood simply as a herald or a religious Paul Revere. He did much more than that. He was also a preacher of truth, and the nature of his preaching was to alert the people to the coming of Christ. His preaching is still of age-long and universal significance.

Once some things are said, that is all there is to it. You can put it down as history, and it has no meaning for anybody following. The preaching of John the Baptist was of age-long significance, because until Christ comes back, and the glory of the Lord is revealed in all places, and the millennium is set up, John's preaching has binding moral application to us all.

John's message was that the kingdom of the Lord was coming and that the King Himself was coming. He was coming to fulfill the ancient prophecies made by Moses and all of the other holy prophets since the world began. John, in announcing the King's coming just behind him, reached out and gathered up all the ancient prophecies about Christ as being everything the human race and the human heart could want.

He presented Christ as the sun shining to light the traveler's way, to warm the earth and brighten the landscape. He was to come as the star of the morning, and He would be the star that would rise and meet His people in their way. He was coming as the Shepherd to lead His sheep in the desert to a green pasture where the still waters were still and sweet. He was coming as a physician to heal the hearts of men. He came as a priest to forgive, to grant complete freedom and to personally offer the sacrifice. He was all that and so much more.

Take your Bible, and on every page, in every verse, you will encounter some bit of gold. You will notice some new wonderful thing that our Lord Jesus is and that He was to come riding upon His chariot.

But the Lord would not come to a wilderness unless there was a satisfactory way prepared, and God will not prepare that way. That was John's message.

He said there is One coming after me, and He will not come unless you prepare the way. He will not come into the wilderness of your life. He will be riding His shining chariot dispensing light like the sun, healing like a physician and guiding like a Shepherd. He will be all this, and He will dispense it from His shining chariot, but He will not drive His chariot into the tangled wilderness of your immoral lives.

He will not come and build the road. That is the business of the people who invite Him in.

It would be morally and psychologically impossible for God to prepare the way of the Lord. We are to prepare the way of the Lord. "I am coming; get ready for me. I am driving my chariot through; you build the highway." That was the burden of John's message: "the voice of one crying in the wilderness, 'Prepare ye the way of the Lord.'"

If God Himself got out of His chariot and built the way, it would be to violate His own nature and the nature of man. Man himself must prepare the way for the coming of the Lord.

What were the results in Israel of John's message? The results were plain to see. Some prepared the way, and to them He came bringing His light and His health and His healing, saying, "Son, thy sins are forgiven thee," and "Daughter, go and sin no more." He turned the water into wine, stilled the waves, forgave sins, gave hope and encouragement. He did all that to them who believed, because they had prepared the way of the Lord.

Others rejected the exhortation of John, remained blind and hard and refused to receive Christ. They opposed Christ, blasphemed Him and finally crucified Him, for they did not all receive Jesus when He came.

They did not all obey the voice of John. In one place it is written that certain ones had rejected the preaching of

John and so they had frustrated the will of God for them (see Luke 7:24-30). That is what happened to those who would not prepare the way. I suppose they wanted God to do everything.

We are living in a time when God is supposed to do everything. What a peculiar and confused theology buzzes in and out of the heads of people today when God has been reduced to a good-sized man! We become offensively personal and intimate in our dealings with God; we joke about Him and call Him our business partner, our copilot, and what have you. We make light of the high King and Prince of glory when we make someone else more sacredly worthy.

At the same time, we fully expect that He will prepare the way. He will do our repenting for us; He will straighten out our lives; He will undo our evil deeds; He will get right with our neighbors for us; He will pay our debts for us and do everything. John did not teach that. John said He is moving in, but He is moving in on a prepared way, and He is not preparing the way. Therefore, "Prepare ye the way of the Lord to make His paths straight."

That is the teaching of the Bible and has been carried down the years to the churches. If the Lord is ready to move into the lives of every last one of us and be as the sun and the star and the rain and the dew; to be the Shepherd and the priest and the light and the healing, He is ready to move in and be all that to us. But our lives are wilderness.

That is why, as believers, we are not getting what we ought. We are not progressing in our spiritual lives as we should, and we are not living the kind of lives we should be living. We have allowed our lives to become a wilderness.

Even when the Lord moved in the day we first believed on Him, some have left their first love and need to repent again.

The way of the Lord is not smooth, and God cannot move in as He wants to move in. If we are to see the glory of the Lord revealed, we are going to have to prepare a way for the Lord.

## The Wilderness of Your Heart

Four things are wrong with the wilderness, and there are four things we have to do before the chariot of God will ride in.

It lies with you and me whether we are going to do this or not. We can sing about Christmas until we get calluses on our vocal cords, and we can celebrate Christmas just as long and loud as we will; but when it is all over, we may be as barren as when we started. The wilderness and the green briars may grow over your soul, and God may be unable to get to where you are, and He may terminate His victorious progress toward your inner life somewhere out in the borders, because He comes to the crooked ways that are grown over and there is no smooth way.

### Straighten the Paths

The first thing that needs to be done is to make His paths straight. God is not going to run around spirals or corkscrews. Make His paths straight. All crooked ways shall be corrected and made straight.

Everybody knows what that means, and you do not need a Philadelphia lawyer to help you. If you want God to bless you, straighten up your life. If you want to have the joy of the

Lord, straighten up your life. You know what is wrong with you. Lo, the chariot of the Lord shines as it moves forward toward your heart's door and finds there only wilderness. John simply said that the crooked shall be made straight. Straighten it up and God will move in.

You know what it means in your own life. I know what it means in my life. And before the judgment of God we will know what it means. If the Lord is going to move in on us with blessings and revival power, there must be a straightening up of our lives.

**Fill the Valleys**

Then we are to fill up every valley. There are so many valleys in our life that take us down. The valleys need to be filled up so that a path can be made. No ruts and hollows in the way of the chariot, which means the sins of omission must be filled up. What does this mean? It means the things that we do not do. No prayers, no Bible study, no giving, no witnessing, no Communion, no seeking God, no pursuing God—things we do not do. To fill up the hollows, we need to start doing them. The chariot of God cannot move in where there are hollows and rocks.

I know many people whose lives are all wilderness, and they ask what book I would recommend. Books cannot prepare a highway for you. I do not recommend any book except the Book of God. We still have the felonious idea in our minds that when we are backslidden, cold, dry and barren, all we need to do is buy a book.

Others, when they find themselves barren and cold, and God seems to be a million miles away, take a course of study. People come and ask what course I would recommend for them.

We need to stop the things we are doing that are wrong and begin doing the things we are neglecting to do.

If you were to go to a doctor and he diagnosed you with malnutrition, you would not take a class; you would ask your doctor to give you a diet so that you could eat better from now on.

How foolish it will be in the day of Christ when the eyes of Jesus, like burning flames, go into our motives and discover us. How frightening to believe that we have allowed ourselves to become overrun by the wilderness and then say, "I will wait for an evangelist," or "I got to hear this wonderful praying man." People are disappointed when a great saint of God moves into a neighborhood. They expect him to have some pill or capsule filled with amazing power. "Take this, sister." The sister takes it but it does her no good. The things of God are not received that way. God does not give His blessings in trick pills.

What is needed is to undo some things, do the things you are not doing and straighten out your crooked life.

### Destroy the High Places

Then we are to cut down the high places. The mountains and hills need to be brought down. In making a railroad, instead of going up over the bump and down into the hollow, they just knock off the bump and fill up the hollow. Some high places in our lives need to be removed to make sure the path is straight. High places of prominence and fame and fortune hinder God coming into your life in victory.

## Smooth the Rough Places

We also need to make the rough ways smooth through humility and obedience, and then we shall see the salvation of God. They take away the rough things and smooth out the road so that the chariots can run over it.

I do not know quite whether I believe it is possible or within the will of God to have a universal revival around the world. I do know it is entirely possible to have a personal revival. I know that you can have that; and if people have personal revivals it could develop into a universal revival.

Let me ask you some questions. Are you satisfied with the way you lived last week? Are you really satisfied with that? Are you satisfied with the degree of light and power and fellowship and purity of your life? Are you truly satisfied?

You can have a personal revival by just doing four little things: Straighten up; begin to do the things you are not doing and should be doing; stop doing things that pop up here and tear down there; take the rocks out and smooth up the highway. Then the shining chariot of God can move into your life.

Anybody can have a personal revival. To start, I recommend getting on your knees somewhere with a pad of paper and pencil. Write down the things that have grieved God, and forsake them forever. Promise Him to do the things you have been neglecting to do. Straighten up that crooked thing in your life and by humility smooth the highway for God, and you shall see the salvation of God before the morning sun rises.

*O God, I beseech Thee to grant me the vision to see, the courage to take advantage of it and the faith to act on it. I will smooth the way by repentance and humility and meekness of spirit. God, help me today, I pray, in Jesus' name, amen.*

# 16

# THE MAN WHO SAW GOD ON THE THRONE

*In the year that King Uzziah died I saw also the Lord sitting upon a throne, high and lifted up, and his train filled the temple.*

ISAIAH 6:1

T his passage from Isaiah is charged with a sense of the holy, of something wholesome, healing and mysteriously profound. It cannot be understood, only felt; only experienced.

The one who cannot feel it—a base soul chained to the earth—is described this way: "And he said, Go, and tell this people, Hear ye indeed, but understand not; and see indeed, but perceive not. Make the heart of this people fat, and make their ears heavy, and shut their eyes; lest they see with their eyes, and hear with their ears, and understand with their heart, and convert, and be healed" (Isa. 6:9-10).

The thing that made Isaiah the voice of God in his generation, and for generations to come, for that matter, was the fact that he saw God. Here Isaiah is trying to express that which we must admit is inexpressible. He is trying to utter that which cannot be uttered, which is said by the theologians to be the ineffable.

In trying to express what he sees, Isaiah is limited by at least three factors.

What he saw was wholly other than and altogether different from anything he had ever seen before. It belonged in a category wholly beyond what he had ever experienced, so he had no "thought stuff" to use to try to understand it.

Likewise, it is impossible for anybody to conceive God. In our singing, praying, worshiping, preaching and thinking, we ought always to draw a sharp line between that which is God and all that is not God. Isaiah had been familiar with that which was not God—all that God had created and made. Up to this time, he had never been introduced into the presence of the Uncreated. The violent contrast between that which is God and that which is not God—the contrast between the Uncreated and the created—was such that language staggered under Isaiah's effort to express it.

If we could grasp God with our intellect, we would be equal to God. We never will be, never can be, equal to God. Therefore, we can never comprehend God with our minds. Yet, Isaiah was trying to do it. He was trying hard to set forth what he saw, and the words were clumsy and inadequate. Words are clumsy and inadequate even when we express that with which we are familiar; so how much less can they express that which is divine.

God was revealing Himself to Isaiah through lofty images. You see, there is a difference between God revealing Himself and man discovering God. Man cannot bore through to God with his intellect. Not all the assembled brains of the world could do it. God can, in one second of time, reveal Himself to the spirit of the man. And so the man knows God, but he knows God experientially, not intellectually.

Everything written here by Isaiah was true, is true, but it is as much greater than what is written as God is greater than the human mind.

Isaiah said, "I saw also the Lord sitting upon a throne" (Isa. 6:1). I wish I could make this vision to be at least dimly seen to all the peoples of the world. God sits upon the throne. We have gotten away from that now. We are afraid it is an evidence of anthropomorphism. (I've never been afraid of big words.) Let them call it what they will, I still believe that God sits upon the throne invested with self-bestowed sovereignty, and that God sits upon the throne determining all issues. That is why I can sleep at night.

Isaiah was encountering the holiness of God. There is a sense of the holy behind all religion, and it is the drive behind every religion in the world. Man has an incurable urge to pray and to worship.

As a result of blindness from sin, this holiness aspect has taken many forms in religion that are grotesque, crude, fantastic, extravagant and vile. The result of this is a lack of truth and purity, and the worship of idols and saints and so forth. It is the response of the human spirit to the mystery, but it is injurious and ineffectual because it is distorted and misdirected by sin.

Man craves that which is holy and tries to manufacture it to satiate his thirst.

To truly understand the holiness of God, we must see him as Isaiah saw him: "sitting upon a throne."

## Man's Response to God's Holiness

Around the throne was the cry, "Holy, holy, holy." From here on, I want to do something that no man ought to attempt to do, so I shall do a poor job of it, I am sure. I want to deal with the word "holy."

### Holy, Holy, Holy

What does the word "holy" mean? It is attributed to the Lord of Hosts here, and it is more than an adjective that says God is a holy God. It is an ecstatic description of glory to the triune God. I am not sure I know what all this means. However, I will offer several words that I believe may come close to them.

Always remember, you can feel your way through to God with your heart long after your mind has given up and quit, because God lies infinitely out yonder, infinitely transcendent above all His creatures. The old Germans used to say, "The heart is always the best theologian." You can know more with your heart than you can with your head.

We may know at least this much: "Holy" meant moral purity. It is good to know there is something left to think about that is absolutely pure. You have to discount everything in the world. A good man is always a good man, but! A good woman is always a good woman, except! Even the saints had their weaknesses and flaws. James—old, severe James—said, "Elijah was a man of like passions as we are" (Jas. 5:17). It is a comforting thing to know that he was a good man, owned by God and, in the sense in which we described, used of God; and yet he was not a perfect man.

Only One is absolutely good; only One is absolutely holy and absolutely morally pure. Only One is righteous, clean, impeccable, faultless and perfect. That One is God. It gives us the feeling of absolute proof to say this in the presence of God.

## Repentance for What We Are

One thing wrong with us today is that we do not repent enough. The reason we do not have more repentance is that we repent for what we do instead of for what we are. The repentance for what you do may go deep, but the repentance for what you are goes deeper. It was the sharp contrast between what God was and what Isaiah was—the absolute holiness of the deity, and the spotted, speckled impurities of Isaiah's nature—that brought this feeling of being absolutely profane to this man of God.

## The Heart Senses What the Mind Cannot

Then it all gives way to mystery that baffles the understanding and stuns the mind, and we come before God in speechless humility in the presence of the mystery inexpressible. I believe we should always leave room for mystery in our Christian faith. When we do not, we become evangelical rationalists and can explain everything. I do not believe we can explain everything. I think there is mystery that runs throughout all the kingdom of God, just as there is mystery running throughout all of the kingdom of nature.

The wisest and the most honest scientist will tell you that he knows practically nothing. The Christian who has met God or seen Him on His throne with the eyes of his heart will stop being an oracle. He will not pretend to know everything, and he will not want to condemn another man who might take a little different position from his.

We must make room for mystery—that mystery that is God. The mystery that cannot be so fluent. When I hear a man pray too fluently, I know he is not seeing anything. His ability to express himself in prayer, unless a sudden outpouring of the Holy Ghost comes upon him, would be able to pray only just average; when we are praying too fluently we are not seeing much.

### Realization of a Terrifying Majesty

When we have seen God on the throne, we also experience a sense of fearfulness. Something portentous and dreadful and terrifying is there. There is a passage in the book of Isaiah written by the same man where he asked the question, "Who among us shall dwell with everlasting burnings?" (Isa. 33:14).

I have heard preachers use this passage to preach on hell and ask the congregation who is going to hell. You could not miss it any further if you tried. The fact is, this is not talking about hell, for it answers its own question. It says, "He that walketh righteously, and speaketh uprightly; he that despiseth the gain of oppressions, that shaketh his hands from holding of bribes, that stoppeth his ears from hearing of blood, and shutteth his eyes from seeing evil" (Isa. 33:15).

In the book of Ezekiel, the first chapter, Ezekiel sat by the River Chebar, despondent and dejected. God opened the heavens, and Ezekiel saw God; and then coming out of the fire, he saw four creatures. We Christians should be men and women out of the fire.

We should be perfectly normal and sound. We should cultivate a sense of humor. We should be perfectly down to earth and as practical as James. Then again, we should have the topside of our souls open to mystery. We should have a window above open to the mystery that is God. Every Christian should be a walking miracle and never be the kind of person who can be explained.

God is holy; and because He is holy, He is actively hostile toward sin. He must be. God can only burn on and burn on and burn on against sin forever. Never let any spiritual experience or any interpretation of Scripture lessen your hatred for sin. It was sin that brought the ruin of the race; it was sin that brought the Savior to die on the cross; it is sin that has filled every jail and hospital and insane asylum. It is sin that has made every murder and every divorce and every crime that has been committed since the world began. In the presence of this awful, holy God, sin can never be anything but a devious deformity.

## "Undone" Before the Throne

Isaiah was not having a vision; Isaiah was seeing something that was there. There is a difference between imagining something to be there and actually seeing what is there. If we had our eyes open, we, too, would see God, because God is everywhere.

### In No Strange Land
Francis Thompson (1859–1907)

The kingdom of God is within you
The angels keep their ancient places—
Turn but a stone and start a wing!
'Tis ye, 'tis your estranged faces,
That miss the many-splendored thing.

It is our faces that have turned from God, missing the many-splendored thing. Isaiah saw this God—the God of Abraham, Isaac and Jacob, and he cried, "I am undone." Here is what someone called self-depreciation to the form of total devaluation.

I am afraid that we are going to try to go out and convert the world by techniques and methods. I am afraid that, unconsciously, we are going to go out and say, "I can do it."

No, my brother, you cannot do it. There are not enough institutions of learning in the world, if you could go through them all and learn everything that can be learned, and read every book that has ever been written; there is not enough knowledge in the world that will enable you to do the job the Holy Ghost is sending you out to do.

He will use your skills and gifts. I believe that all right. He will work through them. But never can you do it by yourself. You have to be "undone." The man whom God uses is the man who is undone. The man who sees God sitting upon the throne is "undone."

Isaiah was awestruck, and his whole world suddenly dissolved into a vast eternal whiteness. He said, "Mine eyes have seen the King."

What kind of a man was Isaiah, anyhow? Was he a criminal, a murderer, a drunkard or a liar? No. He was not any of those things. He was a fine young cultured fellow, cousin to the king, a poet in his own right. He was a good man, and I wish by nature that I was half as good.

In the end, what is the purest morality over against the holiness of the unspeakably holy God? That is what was wrong with Isaiah. When he cried out, "I am undone," he meant that he was experiencing the "undoneness" of the creature set over against the holiness of the Creator.

I do not like the kind of evangelism that gets people in by cards. I think there ought to be a cry of pain. There ought to be a birth from within. I feel there should be the terror of seeing ourselves in violent contrast to the holy, holy, holy God. And if it does not go that deep, I do not know how deep our repentance will ever go. And if our repentance does not go deep, our Christian experience will not go deep.

Here was a man crying out in pain, not for what he had done, for he did not mention a single sin. It was for what he was himself. He was a fallen human being; he was such that he knew he could never venture into the presence of this awesome God. So he cried out, "I am undone."

## Awareness of Our Depravity

The question is not whether we have Isaiah's uncleanness or not. The question is whether we have his awareness. He was unclean, and thank God, he became aware of it. The world today is unclean but unaware of it. Uncleanness with unawareness has terrible consequences, and that is what is wrong with the world. That is what is wrong with the church today. That is what is wrong with Protestantism. We are unclean without being aware.

Uncleanness without any awareness makes us bold and self-assured. It gives us a mistaken conception of our own holiness. It creates false confidence and keeps the doorway to hope shut. When we see God on the throne in the eyes of our heart, and we are blessed by faith and inward illumination to behold a little of how holy God really is, there never will be any question about depravity.

When Isaiah cried out, "I am undone," God said to the Seraphim, "Go." The Seraphim leapt down and pressed the coal to Isaiah's lips.

This man was purified. His lips, symbolic of his nature, were purified by fire. "Now," said God, "thine iniquity is taken away." This is what is called a sense of restored moral innocence. Isaiah knew he was bad, but now he had a sense of moral innocence restored.

Oh, the wonder of the grace of God! We can know how bad we are at the same time that we have gone through this terrifying and humiliating experience—after we have gone through it, and the coal of fire has touched our lives, and we have confessed our deep iniquity and acknowledged how bad we are, not our sins committed but our sin uncommitted. The fire of God's grace touches us, and we have that sense of restored moral innocence.

The forgiving love of God can restore it to us, and then we can serve Him. God said, "Whom shall I send, and who will go for us?"

Then Isaiah said, "Send me." There was the man God was going to use as a voice to his generation. There was the man whose iniquity was taken away.

*Oh God, show a vision of Thyself that will devalue us to the point of total devaluation and from there raise us up and send us forth so that we can go and tell this people. Amen and amen.*

# 17

# JESUS,
# THE LAST PROPHET,
# THE LAST VOICE

*God, who at sundry times and in divers manners spake in time
past unto the fathers by the prophets, hath in these last days spoken
unto us by his son, whom he has appointed heir of all things,
by whom also he made the worlds.*

HEBREWS 1:1-2

Down through history God's prophets have been His voice to His people. No prophet ever originated his own message or even called himself to the work of a prophet. These prophets were men uniquely called of God, not because of who they were but because they were willing to be used of God and meet His conditions.

God will use any man who is willing to be used of God in God's way.

Today we have too many who volunteer their talents to be employed in the cause of God's work. God does not work in that way. God cannot use our talents in and of themselves.

The talents we have, which have been given by God, are simply platforms from which God can act. The talent is not an end in itself.

All the prophets have been different from each other. Even Elijah and Elisha, although similar in some regards, were altogether different men and were used by God according to God's purposes.

Two things brought these prophets together. They were different in many ways, and coming from a vast assortment of backgrounds, two things were quite significant in their ministry as a prophet.

They were a voice to their generation and the uniting factor was the source of that voice. It was not their voices projecting into their culture; rather, it was the voice of God coming through the man who had yielded himself completely to God for this work of a prophet.

Down through the years, the personalities changed from prophet to prophet, but the voice was always the same. It was the voice of a prophet delivering God's message to God's people.

If we would analyze the lives of these prophets and the work they did and the problems they addressed, we would see that what they faced on the surface seems quite diverse. The circumstances were different for each setting. But this is only the surface. When you get down into the work of every prophet, you will find a common thread.

They had a common voice, which came from God, and they were facing common problems among God's people. Regardless of which situation it was, the prophet's voice was directed toward those things; and many times, those things were idols that separated Israel from Jehovah.

The focus of these prophets was always upward. The message came from up above, and the purpose was to draw the attention of the people to the One who sits above the mountains. Their focus was on the God of Abraham, Isaac and Jacob. Although the fathers were gone, the God of the fathers was still on the throne.

The problem each generation faced was that something had come between Israel and God.

It started with the declaration of Lucifer: "I will ascend above the heights of the clouds; I will be like the most High" (Isa. 14:14). This is the epitome of rebellion against God. This declaration has echoed from that time until this time.

The rebellion was introduced into humanity at the Garden of Eden, creating the fall of man: "Now the serpent was more subtle than any beast of the field which the Lord God had made. And he said unto the woman, Yea, hath God said, Ye shall not eat of every tree of the garden?" (Gen. 3:1). This began the great rebellion against God and His Word.

It was brought even to the temptation of Jesus in the wilderness: "And the devil said unto him, If thou be the Son of God, command this stone that it be made bread" (Luke 4:3).

To which our Savior responded, "It is written."

This is the greatest challenge of our generation. The enemy desires to squelch the voice of God, and we need men and women of God to stand against this and be a voice to our generation and shout, "It is written!"

# The Complete Fulfillment
# of All Prophecy

When we come to Jesus Christ, in the New Testament, we come to God's final voice to His people. God "hath in these last days spoken unto us by His Son." His is the last word.

The thing we need to focus on is the fact that every voice from every prophet was directed forward to Jesus Christ and His fulfillment. Every prophecy had its fulfillment in the Lord Jesus Christ. If we are to understand the voice of the prophets, we need to understand what, or maybe I should say, Who they were talking about.

I am not entirely sure that all of the prophets understood where this was going. I think Daniel did, and I am quite sure that Isaiah understood it more than the rest of them. But the voice of the prophets was a matter of obedience. Although the circumstances were different in each case, their obedience was the way of life that led them to Christ, who was the fulfillment of all their prophecy.

God coordinated the many voices into one voice, and that last voice, which was Jesus Christ, was the culmination of all voices.

# The Voice that Brought
# Mankind and God Together

Jesus testified of Himself, "I am Alpha and Omega, the beginning and the ending, saith the Lord, which is, and which was, and which is to come, the Almighty" (Rev. 1:8). This was not just some poetic, religious jargon. Jesus Christ was claiming to be the beginning and the ending of all things, and of everything in between. That which the prophets spoke of back in the early days of time found fulfillment in the Christ to come.

Paul says about this Christ:

> For by him were all things created, that are in heaven, and that are in earth, visible and invisible, whether *they be* thrones, or dominions, or principalities, or powers: all things were created by him, and for him: And he is before all things, and by him all things consist. And he is the head of the body, the church: who is the beginning, the firstborn from the dead; that in all *things* he might have the preeminence. For it pleased *the Father* that in him should all full-ness dwell (Col. 1:16-19).

Every prophecy had its fulfillment in Jesus Christ, and none could be fully understood apart from Him. None of the prophecies molded the character and expectation of Christ; He is the one who molded the prophecies from the very be-ginning. In Revelation we read, "The Lamb slain from the foundation of the world" (Rev. 13:8). The voice of the proph-ets is authenticated in Jesus Christ who truly holds the last word. As the fulfillment of all prophecy, Jesus Christ stands unchallenged before a world of rebellious men and women undaunted by their rebellion.

The prophet Hosea explains this, "And by a prophet the Lord brought Israel out of Egypt, and by a prophet was he preserved" (Hos. 12:13). Those prophets were the foreshad-owing of Jesus Christ. He is the One the prophet is writing about. He is the One who brought Israel out of Egypt and preserved Israel even unto this day. All of the prophets were carrying the voice of God to the people of God.

John begins his gospel with, "In the beginning was the Word, and the Word was with God, and the Word was God" (John 1:1).

In his first epistle, John expounds on this even further: "That which was from the beginning, which we have heard, which we have seen with our eyes, which we have looked upon, and our hands have handled, of the word of life" (1 John 1:1).

What will all the Scriptures tell us about Christ as the fulfillment of all prophecy?

## The Prophets Spoke a Consistent Theme

I think it would have to be the consistency of the theme of the prophets down through the years. In order to understand what they were saying and the overarching aspect of the message, you need to see and focus in on Jesus Christ. No matter where they were or what they were talking about, the focus of their voice was Christ.

No other theme reverberates more than this one. I honestly believe that this theme will be reverberating throughout eternity. I believe Christ begins before time, and time is only a fraction, a temporary aspect. If we want to understand who this Christ is, we must look at Him in the first chapter of Revelation.

It is the theme of Christ who is the supreme ruler over all things. He is the Creator, the Redeemer and the Sustainer of all life. Every prophet's voice was focused in this direction, that Jesus Christ was simply the answer.

We, of course, have the advantage of looking back. Hindsight is always 20/20, as they say. We can see how the puzzle fits together after the puzzle is completed. But these men of God who became the voice of God in their generations walked by faith and not by sight. They were not putting together a puzzle. They were surrendering themselves in absolute obedience to God. Therefore, the remarkable aspect of the voice of the prophet is the consistency of their focus.

The clash of the prophets was between the ideal and the actual. The people to whom they brought the message believed they were okay. They bought into the idea that if they had pleasant thoughts everything would be all right. Indeed, such is the case today. If you keep positive thoughts in your mind, so we are told, you will have a positive outcome in your life. Nobody wants a prophet to come and bring reality into his or her life.

The authenticity of this voice of God was in the reality of the message. When Jesus Christ speaks as the last prophet, He brings into the situation a sense of reality that counters all the superficial ideology we possess today.

## The Prophets Were Attacked and Misunderstood

I think it is safe to say that all of these prophets, including the Lord Jesus Christ, were misunderstood and attacked. All of them had critics, hindrances, gossipers. I do not believe anybody had a worse opponent than Jesus Christ with Judas Iscariot.

The voice of a prophet is always aimed at the false religion among the true religion. Every prophet bristled with denunciation and judgment. They constantly drew a contrast between the false and the true.

Look at Elijah on that mountain with all of the Baal prophets. Elijah stood alone against the false. It takes a man of courage to do this and it is not something you can muster up on your own. There was something in these prophets, like Elijah, that made them men of their generation. Many of them were not accepted; most of them were martyrs to their message.

Every prophet martyred was a prophecy fulfilled in Jesus Christ on the cross. All of their rejection was fulfilled in Jesus Christ.

Every prophet in the Old Testament looked forward to Jesus Christ, whereas today we look back to that cross where He died. We are not serving a dead Christ, but one who is alive forevermore. The fact that He could not be killed gives us the authenticity of His message. The resurrection of Jesus Christ proved that what He said and what He taught was absolutely true.

## The Final Prophetic Voice Still Speaks

We can go forward now in the power and demonstration of the Holy Spirit because Jesus Christ, the final voice of God, is alive forevermore. We do not find Christ in the dusty annals of history. We find Christ in the hearts of every redeemed man, woman and child. He is alive forevermore, and His voice resonates within the heart of every believer.

When Jesus died on the cross, the enemies of God thought they had silenced forever the voice of God. I am so thankful they were wrong. They had three days to rejoice in their victory, but on the third day it came to an end. Jesus Christ rose victorious over all enemies, call them what you will, and is alive forevermore. His message goes on and on and on forever.

## Believers Continue the Message

One of the last things Jesus said to His disciples before His ascension into heaven was, "Go ye therefore, and teach all nations, baptizing them in the name of the Father, and of the Son, and of the Holy Ghost: teaching them to observe all things whatsoever I have commanded you: and, lo, I am with you always, even unto the end of the world. Amen" (Matt. 28:19-20).

Our message to the world was given to us by Christ. The message goes on; Christ is alive today. Because Christ lives, the message lives on in the power of His resurrection.

All of the prophets' messages come together in the Lord Jesus Christ; and the message of Christ is filtered through believers. We now have the final voice that we carry to a world that desperately needs to hear, "Thus saith the Lord." That is the only message that carries with it the unction of the Holy Spirit.

If every prophet was a voice in his generation, and if Christ is the ultimate, final voice, we now carry that voice to our generation in the power and demonstration of the Holy Spirit.

*Oh, Lord Jesus Christ, Thy voice so resonates in our hearts today that we cannot help but go into all the world and be a channel of Thy gospel. This we do in Thy precious name, amen.*

# 18

# THE LADDER INTO KINGDOM POWER

*Be thou exalted, O God, above the heavens:*
*let thy glory be above all the earth.*

PSALM 57:11

David, thank God, was in trouble most of the time; and the way he got out is the way we can get out today. You can learn more from a man who fails than from a man who succeeds if the failure brings him to surrender to God.

David had just escaped from Achish the king of Gath and had fled to that famous cave of Adullam. The men who followed him are described as "everyone that was in distress, and everyone that was in debt, and everyone that was discontented" (1 Sam. 22:2). These are all the men who did not fit in anywhere, and they gathered around David.

David was in trouble, and being the poet that he was, he put everything into vivid figures: "My soul is among Lions: and I live even among them that are set on fire, even the sons of men, whose teeth are spears and arrows, and their tongue a sharp sword" (Ps. 57:4). This is how David describes his dilemma. His enemies had dug pits and booby-traps everywhere for David, and he was in real difficulty.

The color of a man is seen when he is in deep distress and everything is against him. What a person does in that situation really says what kind of a person he is.

David, being a God-taught man, a man after God's own heart, did not make the mistake that many people do. He did not pray, "O God, exalt me. God, show the people that I am Thy servant. Lift me up above my enemies." Who would have blamed David for praying such a prayer? Yet, David understood the reality of his situation and prayed a completely different prayer.

"Be thou exalted, O God, above the heavens: let thy glory be above all the earth."

David knew that the worst thing that could happen to him was for him to be exalted. He understood that would be a treacherous shortcut to victory. He knew that if he put God between him and his troubles, his troubles would dissolve and he would get out all right without any harm. Therefore, he began to pray to God that God might exalt Himself above the heavens.

In this, David was theologically sound. When God created the heaven and the earth, He made it to be like this. He, God, was to be first. He was to be first in sequential order, as He certainly is—the first cause and above all in rank and station, exalted in dignity and honor. He was to have first place in the hearts of all moral creatures. This is the way God created the heavens and the earth.

It was not an arbitrary thing on God's part. He did not say, "I am going to create me a world to praise me." God being who He is and what He is had to be first. In creating moral beings and an environment for them to live in, it had to be according to the nature of God. His glory must be above all the heavens.

## God's Glory Supreme

The one essential thing we need to remember is that the glory of God is our chief objective in life, not the winning of souls. The winning of souls always comes second to the glory of God. But God, being who He is and the kind and loving God that He is, has so arranged it that the more He is glorified, the more people are saved. So, it works better to glorify God first.

The first prayer was, "Hallowed be Thy name." For God to be exalted, for us to put God up first, we must let God have first place in our thinking; we must let Him have first place in our giving, and first place in our lives, our homes, our business, our profession. God must be first in your life. The triune God is supreme in all things. This supremacy restores the health of the universe, for the trouble with the fallen world is that it is inverted. God is made to take second place. He never actually takes second place, but He is made to take it in the minds of fallen men, and they are exalting themselves all the time. If they give a dollar to the Red Cross, they wear a red feather showing that they have given a dollar. We are always exalting ourselves. The result is that God is always given second place, and this is always unhealthy. It brings disease to all the parts of the world that it touches.

The purpose of God in redemption is to restore that right order, bringing health to the entire universe. God sits on the throne alone, and everybody's heart is to know that there is the throne. Either God sits on it or man sits on it. The trouble with the world is that every man sits on his own throne.

Isaiah defined for us the essence of sin: "All we like sheep have gone astray; we have turned every one to his own way; and the Lord has laid on him the iniquity of us all" (Isa. 53:6). The key phrase is that "we have turned every one to his own way." The turning to my own way instead of God's way is the essence of sin. It is rebellion, unbelief, selfishness and self-will all rolled into one.

That is what is wrong with the world today, that is what is wrong with the United Nations, and that is what is wrong with the West. God gets no place, or if He does, it is second, third or fourth place.

David, finding himself in a jam, knew that the way to get out was to begin to put God where He belongs. David's giving God first place in his heart and in his mind came to David's defense.

This is where we need to start. What place does God have among us?

Those who call themselves by the name of Christ and pray to Him a certain amount are content in their position; but the true place in the heart is always found, not by what we say, but by what we do.

Let me put forth a few penetrating questions.

Usually when we get up feeling grouchy, we preach against the liberals. I think it was Oliver Wendell Holmes who said, "Feeling bad this morning; liver troubling me. Decided to stay in bed and write a thesis on total depravity."

That is a grouchy theology, so I am not focusing my remarks on the liberals.

Let me focus on those of us who call ourselves evangelicals, those of us who believe in the historic Christianity and the Bible as the inspired Word of God.

### Consider Your Personal Finances

When it comes to a choice between God and money, where does God rate a rule? Most people tithe because they have learned it is economically profitable to tithe. People will say that they go further on their 9/10 than they did on their 10/10. Any businessman would give a tithe immediately if he knew he would come out better.

### Consider Your Personal Ambitions

What about our ambition and our fleshly enjoyment? How do we rationalize our ambition and appease ourselves and give God second place?

When it comes to a choice between God and marriage, who wins? God, or the young lady? God, or the young man?

When it comes to a choice between God and our friends, and especially when it comes to a choice between God and self, who wins?

I believe this is why evangelical churches are staggering on, because we will not give God the place that is His by right of who He is and who we are. Whenever human will enters in, this monstrous inversion is found. Out in the world of nature, up among the stars, everything is all right because they have no will. As soon as we get where God wants us, we have trouble.

There's no trouble among the angels, because they are not fallen; but among fallen men and devils and many other creatures who have moral perception, there is always this monstrous inversion. God always gets second place or third place or tenth place, while other things are put above Him. And yet, at the same time, these persons, who put God below them, may be extremely religious.

There will be no inward peace until God is exalted over us and we are abased. We can read all the books in the world and we can read the Scriptures through once a year and sing our way through the hymnal, but when it is all over, we will never find peace or victory until God is given the place in our hearts that He has in the universe.

This truth runs through all the teachings of Jesus Christ our Lord. "If any man would come after me, let him take up his cross and follow me" (Matt. 16:24). Unfortunately, we have made taking up the cross to be a very poetic thing. Taking up the cross meant that we would stop making plans. The man who took up the cross in the old Roman days did not have any plans. Someone else made his plans for him.

Someone came to an old man of God and asked, "You teach the deeper life, the life lost in God. Tell me, what does it mean to be crucified with Christ?"

The old man scratched his head a little, gathered his thoughts and then said, "The crucified man only faces one direction. He is not facing all around, but only facing one direction. The second thing about a crucified man, he has no plans of his own; somebody else is making all his plans for him."

These are the days of projects and enterprises and ambitions from little fellows who have not stayed in Jerusalem long enough to be endued with power. They go out in the power of educated flesh and put on a project, and then ask God to bless their project. They even will pray all right. They will send out a mailing list to enlist people to pray such and such an hour for their project. It is their project nevertheless. They have not died yet! They are making their plans.

My brother, when you go to a cross, you do not make your own plans. Somebody else is making those plans for you. So when God makes your plans, and you forsake all, even house and land and family, you have to forgo all of this and put God first.

## The Climb Toward Deep Spiritual Satisfaction

What is the Holy Spirit trying to tell us here? Let me offer you a ladder upon which you can climb into the kingdom of power. I want to offer you the secret that will bring you riches and inward experiences such as you have never had before. This is the secret that will bring you to deep spiritual satisfaction for your total nature, usefulness, fruitfulness and growth such as you have never known before. In addition, it will bring you the ravishing knowledge of the only true God.

To begin with, I believe in personal communion with God to the point of incandescence. I believe that we should fellowship with God until, like Moses, some of the glow of God is upon our faces.

David understood the secret, which is to exalt God over ourselves, at any cost to us, and always put God first. We are to put God where He belongs. God always keeps safe everything you give to Him, and you always jeopardize everything you hold on to.

You need to exalt God above your friendships. Give up your friend that you might have the Friend; but we hang on to our friends and we know the Friend only very poorly and inadequately.

"Be thou exalted, O God," over my comforts and over my pleasures. Some people spend so much time taking vacations that they call it recreation. They say they are taking a vacation, and I say, a vacation from what? Mostly it is a vacation from nothing more strenuous than loafing, but it is supposed to be re-creating something or other. We put our pleasures and our comforts first and then God takes what's left.

Be thou exalted above my ambitions. I like to see ambitious Christians, but I want to know whose ambition is interesting them.

I appreciate the old German preacher, the medieval theologian and mystic Meister Eckhart. While others may find him shocking, I like him. He once preached a sermon on Jesus and the moneychangers. At the root of his sermon was the thought that these men were serving God for a profit, which is what got the anger of Jesus against them, and He drove them from the place. They were doing religious work that should have been done, but they were doing it for a profit. There are those who would not open the door in the house of God except for profit. I count any man who serves God for profit to be a huckster and a moneychanger. I fully concur with the old German preacher.

The profit I am talking about here is not necessarily financial profit. Most of us do not have much to worry about in that regard, but there is another kind of profit we like to get. We serve God on commission. It is a very low commission, and the more spiritual we are the lower the commission we are willing to take for the work we do. We want to serve God, but we want a commission. "Oh God, we will give Thee 95 percent of the glory, but could we have 5 percent?" Then we get blessed at some revival meeting, and say to God, "Oh Lord, let it be 3 percent." But God says, "I am Jehovah. That is My name, and My glory will I not give to another." God will not give His glory to anybody. A day will come when He will allow us to share all of His glory with Him, but that day is not now.

Now we are to bear crosses, to do without, to lose our goods, to be frowned upon. Now we are called to be a minority group, a despised minority group. This idea that you can make the cross of Christ sociably acceptable is a heresy of our generation. Many evangelical groups are trying to prove to the world that we are not so dumb after all. We amount to something. We are somebody now in our own right, and we believe in Jesus, too.

You might as well quit. As soon as the disgrace of the cross is out of your life, the power goes out of your life. Just as soon as you are no longer a despised minority group, you are not a powerful people.

We like to keep our reputation elevated, and I always have to try to die to my reputation. It is odd, that which you do not have is what you have to die to. I have to go to God constantly and die to my reputation. I like what Vance Havner said: "Don't imagine you're a big wheel just because you have a shiny hubcap." We are always finding some fellow with a shiny hubcap and we push him up. Even we Protestants have to have our saints to venerate.

John the Baptist had it right when he said, "He must increase and I must decrease" (John 3:30). God can always use a man if He knows His glory is safe in that man's hands.

When doing research for my biography of A. B. Simpson, I talked to William T. MacArthur, who was a personal friend and coworker with him. He told me many things about Dr. Simpson that I had not known before. Finally, I asked MacArthur, "If this man was so imperfect, why did God bless him as He did?"

MacArthur straightened up, stroked his beard and said, "God knew that His glory was safe in the hands of Albert Simpson."

God will bless any man when He knows His glory is safe in his hands; but He will hold back His blessing and give it only in measure when He has reason to believe that that man wants a percentage of the glory. When that man has not settled that God is above all, he limits what God can do for him.

It is hard to comprehend this since we are living in the age of religious Adam. You can see him everywhere; just scratch him and he gets mad. As long as you do not oppose him, he can be as religious as you can imagine. We are living in a very breezy, self-contained Christianity.

Look at the roster of the spiritually successful. I do not need to list them here; you know who they are. This was their secret: "Be thou exalted, O God, over me. Have first place in my life and let me take what is left. Be Thou above me, O God. Exalt Thyself at my expense; at any cost be Thou exalted, O God."

Somebody said it this way: "'My kingdom go' is a necessary correlator of 'Thy kingdom come.'" Until your kingdom goes, His kingdom cannot come. We will never be where we ought to be until this happens. The King has to be first; and the assistant kings and junior kings and little kings reigning down, but there can only be one King in any one kingdom. If the kingdom in your heart can have only one King, it is either you or Jesus Christ. Has He been the King, or have you been the king over the past day?

Some people will object and say, "Oh, I pray daily that God will help me."

Yes, help you to be a good king. But have you ever stopped to think that you need to get down off that throne and ask God Almighty to forgive you for ever sitting on it? Have you ever thought about just changing your prayer and saying, "Take it, Lord. Exalt Thyself. Take thy throne and reign."

*Lord Jesus, Thou art exalted above all. Help us at any cost to ourselves to put the crown on Thy forehead and give Thee the scepter. I ask this in Jesus Christ our Lord, amen.*

# 19

# PRAYER OF A PROPHET

*O LORD, I have heard thy speech, and was afraid: O LORD, revive thy work in the midst of the years, in the midst of the years make known; in wrath remember mercy.*

*God came from Teman, and the Holy One from mount Paran. Selah. His glory covered the heavens, and the earth was full of his praise. And his brightness was as the light; he had horns coming out of his hand: and there was the hiding of his power. Before him went the pestilence, and burning coals went forth at his feet. He stood, and measured the earth: he beheld, and drove asunder the nations; and the everlasting mountains were scattered, the perpetual hills did bow: his ways are everlasting. I saw the tents of Cushan in affliction: and the curtains of the land of Midian did tremble.*

*Was the LORD displeased against the rivers? was thine anger against the rivers? was thy wrath against the sea, that thou didst ride upon thine horses and thy chariots of salvation? Thy bow was made quite naked, according to the oaths of the tribes, even thy word. Selah. Thou didst cleave the earth with rivers. The mountains saw thee, and they trembled: the overflowing of the water passed by: the deep uttered his voice, and lifted up his hands on high. The sun and moon stood still in their habitation: at the light of thine arrows they went, and at the shining of thy glittering spear. Thou didst march through the land in indignation, thou didst thresh the heathen in anger. Thou wentest forth for the salvation of thy people, even for salvation with thine anointed; thou woundedst the head out of the house of the wicked, by discovering the foundation unto the neck. Selah. Thou didst strike through with his staves the head of his villages: they came out as a whirlwind to scatter me: their rejoicing was as to devour the poor secretly. Thou didst walk through the sea with thine horses, through the heap of great waters. When I heard, my belly trembled; my lips quivered at the voice: rottenness entered into my bones, and I trembled in myself, that I might rest in the day of trouble: when he cometh up unto the people, he will invade them with his troops.*

*Although the fig tree shall not blossom, neither shall fruit be in the vines; the labour of the olive shall fail, and the fields shall yield no meat; the flock shall be cut off from the fold, and there shall be no herd in the stalls: Yet I will rejoice in the LORD, I will joy in the God of my salvation. The LORD God is my strength, and he will make my feet like hinds' feet, and he will make me to walk upon mine high places.*

*To the chief singer on my stringed instruments.*
—Habakkuk 3:2-19

# Books by A. W. Tozer